ABOUT THE AUTHOR

MARIA CIONI was born in Calgary, Alberta, the answer to her parents' prayers and a distraction for her older brother, Gary, who had begged for either a sister or a dog. From ages three to nine she lived at La Villa, with cats and customers as her friends, the Wurlitzer as her orchestra, and the dance floor as her stage. She completed her bachelor's and master's degrees at the University of Calgary and went on to Cambridge University in England, where she received a doctorate in British history, specializing in Elizabethan law as it pertained to women.

Maria is the principal of Maria Cioni and Associates, a company that provides services in the field of international education to schools, universities, governments, and professional associations in Canada and abroad. She lives with her husband, Mark, and daughter, Rafaela, in Toronto, but Calgary remains her home in her heart.

PHOTO BY RAFY

To my cousin, Lina
Thank you for the stories.
With much love,
Maria

DEDICATION

For Family

SPAGHETTI WESTERN

HOW MY FATHER BROUGHT ITALIAN FOOD TO THE WEST

FIFTH
HOUSE

Cover design by David Drummond
Interior design by Brian Smith / Articulate Eye Design
Edited by Lesley Reynolds
Copyedited by Lori Burwash
Proofread by Geri Rowlatt
Scans by ABL Imaging
Polenta recipe: Valerie Mitchell, *Polenta on the Board*. Victoria, BC: www.polenta.ca, 2003, pp. 26–27.

The type in this book is set in Adobe Jenson.

The publisher gratefully acknowledges the support of The Canada Council for the Arts and the Department of Canadian Heritage.

 Canada Council **Conseil des Arts**
for the Arts **du Canada**

We acknowledge the financial support of the Government of Canada through the Book Publishing Industry Development Program (BPIDP) for our publishing activities.

Printed in Canada by Friesens

06 07 08 09 10 / 5 4 3 2 1

First published in the United States in 2007 by
Fitzhenry & Whiteside
311 Washington Street
Brighton, MA 02135

Library and Archives Canada Cataloguing in Publication

Cioni, Maria L. (Maria Lynn), 1948-
Spaghetti western : how my father brought Italian food to the West / Maria L. Cioni.

ISBN-13: 978-1-897252-02-4
ISBN-10: 1-897252-02-1
1. Cioni, Gene. 2. Cooks—Alberta—Calgary—Calgary—Biography. 3. Cookery,
Italian—Alberta—Calgary—History. 4. La Villa (Restaurant : Calgary, Alta.).
5. Italians—Alberta—Calgary—History. I. Title.
TX649.C54C54 2006   641.5092   C2006-902925-3

Fifth House Ltd.
A Fitzhenry & Whiteside Company
1511, 1800-4 St. sw
Calgary, Alberta T2S 2S5

1-800-387-9776
www.fitzhenry.ca

CONTENTS

PREFACE

Imagine that Italian food did not exist—that spaghetti, ravioli, and chicken cacciatore could not be found on any menu. That was how it was in Calgary before March 1949.

I remember sitting on top of the long, white apron that covered my father's knees, listening to his stories. With his back propped against the wooden pop cases on the La Villa restaurant loading dock, we'd take off on an adventure. "This is a hippoTOMAS," said my father, pointing to the animal in my picture book. Then he closed the book and began his tale of the big grey animal searching the world to find good spaghetti.

Years later in school, I repeated the animal's name and was shocked when my classmates roared with laughter.

"Daddy, the animal is called a hip-po-POT-a-mus." I pronounced it slowly so he could see my lips form the word.

"I know. But I like hippoTOMAS better."

Now, five decades later, I appreciate that my father, Genesio Cioni, always liked to do things his way. An immigrant, he followed his own path, taking risks because he believed in himself and his abilities, and in the limitless possibilities of Canada.

I never fully appreciated the significance of his Italian origins to our family until a few years ago, when I was listening to CBC radio while driving. A guest was telling of how he lived and played above the family store. It hit me that I too had lived above the family business. Until then, I had never equated my La Villa world with an immigrant experience. I was so astounded that I had to pull over to recompose myself.

I realize now that my family life was certainly unique. By the age of seven, I had memorized the lyrics of hundreds of songs on the jukebox. I could cha-cha, jive, and waltz. I sat on the knees of some of Calgary's most eligible bachelors. I learned how to be a hostess, thanks to my mother. I touched the waxed handlebar moustache of a famous wrestler, and I went for spins in a Cadillac convertible, perched on the armrest between driver and passenger.

Yet mine was an immigrant experience like millions of others. "Work hard seven days a week and be respectful" was my father's formula for success, which he happily shared with many new Italian immigrants arriving in Calgary after the war. To them, "Mr. Gene" was an icon, one of the few of his generation to master his fate and succeed in his own business outside the Italian community.

I have come to understand that my father drew customers not only because of his excellent food, but because he personified the essence of Italian culture, welcoming patrons and friends to his restaurant to share the intimacy of food and enjoy one another's company. The Fabulous Fifties was an unforgettable era in oil-rich Calgary, and my father and his restaurants were at the middle of it all. Fifty years later, patrons still reminisce, "What fun we had in those days with Gene at La Villa."

Come sit with me and I'll tell you his story.

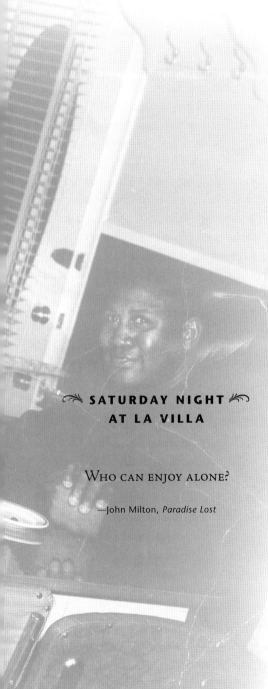

**☙ SATURDAY NIGHT ☙
AT LA VILLA**

WHO CAN ENJOY ALONE?

—John Milton, *Paradise Lost*

|One|

MY FATHER, Gene Cioni, glanced at the clock over the double steel sinks and was uneasy to find that it was only ten o'clock, the night still very young. The hundred Red Brand T-bone steaks bought just that morning might not last. At least forty more customers—football players, wrestlers, and fans—would be joining the throng already dining and dancing at La Villa. My mother, Martha, hostess of the dining room, was miraculously finding space for everyone while ensuring that Stella, the head waitress, was in top form.

Rolling his eyes to the ceiling, Gene thanked God that the cases of spaghetti and crates of Parmesan and Romano cheese had arrived from Toronto before the weekend. Two perpetually bubbling pots of water that steamed windows and staff alike were on standby for the cooked-to-order spaghetti or rigatoni dinners. Tomato sauce perfumed the air as wafts of oregano, basil, garlic, and lemon rose from the grill.

As in my father's two previous restaurants, the kitchen was open. He liked customers to come and chat and watch him prepare food. Gene had introduced Italian cuisine to Calgary five years before, and now, in 1954, he was still presenting patrons with new tastes—tastes cultured by the Romans, distilled through the chromosomes of Abruzzese ancestors, and translated from his cultural memory into feathery light ravioli, al dente spaghetti, pizza pie, and quality Alberta meat prepared in Gene's Italian style to heighten the natural flavour.

"If I ever needed you, I need you now," crooned Eddie Fisher, reminding Gene that customers were waiting for his presence in the dining room. My mother would also be on the lookout for him. Fifteen years of marriage had enabled each to anticipate the other's need. Gene untied the strings of his long, white apron and grabbed two steak dinner platters. Looking over his shoulder, he checked as one helper rubbed herbs on the chicken while the other prepared anchovy salads. Towers of heavy, white plates teetered beside the large sinks as Ruby, the dishwasher, plunged handfuls of silverware into hot, soapy water.

Gene slid a steak platter in front of Sid Gelfand. "Hi, Doc, here's your favourite. How was the drive out?" The question had become their in-joke. Dr. Gelfand had been the first customer to make his way over potholed gravel roads to La Villa on opening day in April 1952.

"I don't know if I ever told you, Gene, but I always know when my colleague is coming here to eat spaghetti and veal. I see him downing a quart of milk to coat his ulcers. He says only your food is worth the suffering!"

"I can't disagree with a doctor," laughed my father.

The other steak was for Adelmo Brandelli, who had lived with two of his brothers in the apartment above Gene's first restaurant. Brandelli was a *paesano*, from the same hometown of Antrodoco. In Italian, my father said, "Your brother Gabriele was in the other night. He brought a couple rhubarb leaves, calling them *scoffulitti*. I'd forgotten that we used *scoffulitti* in the old days, to wipe our bottoms when we washed in the Velino River."

While a waitress began serving the main course to the table, Gene kissed Jean Brandelli, Adelmo's wife, complimenting her black net cocktail dress and rhinestone accessories. He exchanged a little gossip about Calgary with Eva Rebaudengo and her husband, Renaldo, whose uncle had been the honorary Italian consul before the war.

"Look who's here!" Gene shouted with delight when he saw Julio Poscente, now an oil executive, and his wife, Maureen, walking toward the table. During the Depression my father had gone to Trail, British Columbia, where Julio's parents, also from Antrodoco, had nurtured him. Julio had learned over the years that in Gene's restaurants he was never allowed to pay.

Larger parties were seated in the alcoves beside the dance floor. Tonight Gene's nieces, Connie Santopinto and Jean Amantea, had come with sixteen others to enjoy Saturday night at La Villa. He kissed them and pinched their cheeks. Jean snuggled beside her husband, Jack, who with his three brothers, Ralph, Mike, and Frank, owned Amantea Shoes.

While Gene was building his La Villa restaurant, the Amantea brothers were establishing one of the largest family shoe stores in Calgary. With the party was a Franciscan priest and close family friend, Father Timothy Gilcher. A few years earlier, he had cajoled my father to go to the Mount St. Francis Retreat House in Cochrane to cook a spaghetti dinner for the religious community. The dinner had become an annual event, so they set a date for the next one before the chef hurried back to the kitchen to start preparing the waiting orders.

Out in the gravel parking lot, Lynne Hanson exited from a Cadillac with a pirouette (a vestige of her ballerina days) and disappeared into La Villa, while her husband looked for parking. Ten minutes later, Swede Hanson trudged in and spotted his wife in the arms of Ras Mikkelson, her crinolines dipping and twirling to "Three Coins in the Fountain."

"Good evening, Martha. I see that my wife is already enjoying herself!"

"I'll take you to your friends." My mother grinned and hung up his coat.

The hostess directed Swede past a couple of his colleagues in the oil business to where Mena Mikkelson sat sipping whisky and 7-Up with Angus and Margaret McLennan. "I'll bring more 7-Up and tell Gene you're here."

"I'm coming as soon as the veal is ready," Gene advised.

Ras and Mena were still celebrating the sale of their farm. They had known that land values were escalating but never expected the bonanza of a gravel quarry on their property. My father placed a kiss on Mena's cheek and bent to give the other ladies a peck. Then he embraced the men. "I heard the wonderful news about the sale of your farm. Congratulations!"

"We're still overwhelmed," admitted Mena. "A half million dollars!" She lassoed Ras with her brown mink stole and drew him in for a kiss.

"What will you have this evening?" Gene asked.

"Jumbo shrimp cocktails for everyone," Mena replied. "Our treat. We can afford the best."

My father could hear the noise level rising. It was time to get back to the kitchen and have Salina prepare the shrimp cocktails. But as he passed the entrance, he saw Hy and Jenny Belzberg coming in. They often spent Saturday night at La Villa with a large party of friends. He stopped to greet them.

The La Villa dining room after the second renovation, 1953.
Kay Wiley serves a table in the back left, while Stella Volk stands beside
the table in the centre where Mother and I are seated.

Over the years, Belzberg family members had become friends. Hy owned Cristy's Furniture Store, where we bought our art deco furniture and first television set. In the wee hours of the morning, Hy's brother, Bill, partied and sometimes shared his bachelor's angst with Gene. Abraham and Hinda, the elder Belzbergs, enjoyed my father's Italian food, which he specially prepared for them in a kosher way. In fact, Abraham had so enjoyed the Italian food that he proposed Gene open a restaurant on a piece of land that he owned near downtown. My father declined the offer of the self-made millionaire.

In the kitchen, six jumbo shrimp cocktails were started. Gene checked the supply of veal scaloppine, knowing it was a favourite of the Belzbergs, and took out some chicken livers for Jenny. "We're filling fast," he advised the assistants. "Get more salads ready and open another case of spaghetti."

By the time Gene returned to the dining room, the Belzbergs were enjoying their favourite anchovy salads. "We'd like to host a party at La Villa for Shirley and Jack Singer. They're moving to California," said Hy. "You decide the menu, Gene." A few years before, the Belzbergs had hosted a similar event for Harold and Lottie Cohen, who then changed their plans and remained in Calgary.

"I'll serve the lasagna," said my father. "It might convince them to stay!"

My parents knew the rest of the Belzberg table well. Beryl and Leon Libin's Palace Bakery made La Villa's breadsticks; Benjamin Pearlman's company, Polar Aerated Water Works, supplied 7-Up and Crush soft drinks; and Sam Viner was our dentist. Ann and Ralph Kalef, owners of National Department Stores, liked to dance first and eat later. On Sundays, these same couples often returned with their families for a casual dinner, but on Saturday night their children were at home fast asleep, as I was upstairs, being babysat by my brother, Gary.

"Let me know when you're ready for the main course," Gene advised the table.

Martha spotted the moth-eaten buffalo coats and knew that two of her friends had arrived. Their presence meant that the Stampeder football game was over and that fans and players would soon be streaming in. Hazel Dixon, a statuesque, fine-boned model, shed her buffalo skin and bent to kiss the hostess. While they waited for Rolly Bradley, an executive for Crown Assets, to pull a paper bag containing a couple of bottles of beer from the pocket of the smelly coat as he hung them up, Hazel reported that Rolly's mother was nearly finished crocheting a wardrobe for my ballerina doll.

"Who won the game?" my mother asked, seating them at a reserved table.

Gene visiting with Lynne Hanson, 1956.

Dinner at La Villa after a Stampeder game, 1952. Left to right: Bob Paffrath, Rollie Miles, Gene, Sugarfoot Anderson and Bob Mike.

"The Stamps, of course," chuckled Rolly.

Gene had just delivered a couple of plates of spavioli to the Kalefs. He came up, put an arm around his wife's shoulder, and planted a small kiss on Hazel's cheek. My parents loved this couple who, when football season ended, often came to La Villa so early that they ate two dinners in an evening.

"Sugarfoot caught the winning pass," Rolly volunteered as the chef hugged him.

Hazel asked for advice, "Gene, I don't want to eat anything too heavy."

"First, a bowl of homemade soup to warm you up. Then I'm going to bring sautéed chicken livers with onions and green peppers."

My mother had slipped away and returned with a bottle opener, cups and saucers, and teapots, knowing that Rolly liked to decant his beer. He handed her the beer, which she opened and poured into two brown earthenware teapots. She filled their cups and took the beer bottles away. Until 1958, restaurants in Calgary and Edmonton were not allowed to sell liquor. Customers brought their own alcohol discreetly wrapped in brown paper bags, which they placed under the tables. The restaurant provided the glasses and the mix.

Gene had moved on to greet Paul Rowe, the all-star fullback of the 1948 Grey Cup champion Calgary

Stampeders, and his wife, Vivian. Paul had frequented Gene's first restaurant since shortly after it opened and had helped establish its reputation. Now, their gang of thirteen piled into La Villa. Bill Bishop, project manager of the nearby Spruce Cliff Apartments, and his wife, Barbara, were sitting beside Paul. Bill told Gene that soon three more apartment buildings would be finished. "Wonderful, more customers for La Villa!" Gene beamed.

Vivian Rowe's brother, Ross Maguire, was there, too. He claimed that he didn't like Italian food but came to La Villa for the fun and ended up having some of the best meals he had ever eaten. Hal Gooding, the chief pilot for Imperial Oil, told of his adventures around the world, and Ken Russell, the sales manager of a car dealership, and his wife, Dorothy, teased Gene about his love of new cars.

"We have five reservations in the next half hour, forty people," my mother's voice rose above the din in the kitchen. "That doesn't cover the football players and wrestlers that will just turn up. It's going to be tight. I may have to turn people away if they don't want to wait."

"I could run out of steaks," Gene confided. He glanced at the clock again. "The police should be here soon." He slid extra rigatoni into the boiling water.

Moments later, a familiar figure appeared in the kitchen. "I'm starving.

An impromptu consultation in the kitchen between Martha and Gene, 1957.

I've got to eat now. Gene, feed me!" boomed Sugarfoot Anderson, entwining the short cook in his professional football grasp. My father laughed and wriggled loose from his friend.

"I hear you were the star tonight. Find a seat. I'll keep the food coming. Who's with you?"

"A few from the losing team," the big man bellowed.

Sugarfoot's party was seated, but he strolled around the tables. He pulled Paul Rowe over to Red Dutton's table for support and proceeded to assure the Stampeder general manager that a new football stadium would help the team win another Grey Cup. Gene intervened to suggest, "Now that my barn's burned down, you can build a new stadium here and I'll cater the games!"

"Gene, where do you get these ideas from?" laughed Paul.

This cheerful group of Stampeders, and all the other La Villa customers there that night, knew that my parents provided the essentials of enjoyment, Italian style: the best food in town, music, and dancing. The Wurlitzer pumped out Guy Lombardo and his Royal Canadians and the strings of the Percy Faith Orchestra, the songs of Jo Stafford and Perry Como, and the jazz beat of Ella Fitzgerald, Louis Armstrong, and Count Basie. A powdered wax, sprinkled across the hardwood floor every afternoon, removed friction to free the soles. A customer with one leg shorter than the other had found a warped rise in the oak boards. Planting himself on the secret spot, he danced the night away.

A show of black taffeta, strapless cocktail dresses, fur-trimmed brocade sheaths, printed silks, and pastel chiffons swished by on the arms of dark woollen suits. Then Mena Mikkelson pulled the plug of the jukebox and everyone stopped. She stood with her arms wide open and began to sing the Rosemary Clooney hit "Hey There." She moved between the tables, sometimes stopping to wink. The room burst into applause and the music returned.

Some customers left early, and my mother made sure those tables were quickly reset. She gave a passing waitress an empty breadstick cup to refill. Jack and Helen Holdsworth arrived with their friends the Hunts and the Quigleys, from the real estate and insurance businesses, respectively, as well as Bea and Dean Griffing. Jack Holdsworth, a successful jeweller, had played football under Coach Griffing. Hurriedly taking off their coats, Helen announced, "Martha, we want to get right to the dance floor." My mother set aside a table for eight and surveyed the few empty places. She wondered how Gene's steaks were holding out.

"Is there room for us, too?" asked a chorus. Martha stood on the toes of her grey suede pumps for a better view of the door. Just as she thought, a contingent of football players: Eddie LeBaron, Harry Langford, and five other Stampeders. "Good evening, gentlemen. A table is being set for you."

Gene pushed the chicken over to one side of the grill to make room for the last of the steaks. Then he slid veal dipped in egg and home-made bread crumbs into olive oil and butter to sauté. Mary, another assistant, strained orders of rigatoni while Salina sliced onions, peppers, and mushrooms. The kitchen hummed.

A pounding on the back door broke their concentration—the police had arrived. Gene greeted the two officers. "The rigatoni's almost ready, come sit down." Taking off their caps, the burly pair sat at the family table, just outside the kitchen, and started with anchovy salad.

A waitress alerted my mother that the police were eating. "No glasses of liquor on the table. Please tuck your bottle out of sight," she said, gliding between the tables. A few new customers unfamiliar with the drill were given more instruction. "Please finish your drinks imme-diately. Place the bottle on the floor where it can't be seen. Then just act normally." One fellow, who was faint of heart, bolted for the door to hide in his car. Everyone else carried on enjoying themselves.

With their meal finished, the officers rose and put on their hats. They walked into the dining room and stood for a couple of minutes. Some people waved. Martha greeted them and chatted.

"Thanks for dinner, Gene. See you soon."

"Nice to see you boys," he said waving.

Soon after the police left, Martha turned down the overhead lights, leaving only the soft glow from the wall sconces and the flickering light from candles in wicker-clad Chianti bottles. La Villa was now a supper club, with hints of romance and intrigue.

Gene was pan-frying chicken rubbed with garlic and oregano when an American customer rushed into the kitchen. He smiled; she didn't.

"I was enjoying my salad when some Negroes came in. Where I come from we don't eat in the same place. Tell them to leave. Either they go or I will!"

Gene took the customer by the elbow and guided her out of the

The Rowe party at La Villa, April 1957.

kitchen to a quieter corner. "Tell me," he started calmly, though he was shocked by her ultimatum, "you go to the Stampeder football games, don't you?"

"Yes," she huffed.

"They're Stampeders and I'm honoured that they choose to come to my restaurant. Maybe you didn't recognize them without the uniforms. They're sports heroes you pay to watch. Everyone wants to see them. So, you're lucky because tonight you get to eat with them!"

My father was not going to back down. He hoped that his explanation would suffice, but he was also willing to give the American woman more attention and distract her by focusing on food. "Come, I'll take you to your table. Have you ordered a main course yet?" After introducing himself to her husband, he sat down with them. He talked about the menu and suggested various dinner options, promising to cook anything they wished.

Martha noticed her husband sitting and knew immediately that something was up. She hadn't seen this couple before and concluded they must be newcomers to Calgary. Approaching Don McIntosh, a city councillor, she whispered, "Don, may I ask a favour? Would you come and welcome those newcomers?" She introduced the city politician and could see that the couple was flattered by all the attention. Don, a generous person, welcomed their questions about the booming city. Gene excused himself to return to the kitchen.

Soon, sports announcers Ed Whalen and Ted Soskin strolled into the kitchen to greet Gene. My father had bought one of the first television sets in Calgary just to watch Ed interview the wrestlers. Ted mentioned a recent sports column about a wrestler who had been carried out of the ring on a stretcher only to be seen a few hours later enjoying himself at La Villa. "Ya, I think he had veal scaloppine!" laughed my father. "Martha loved the column so much that she clipped it out and taped it above the telephone."

Stu Hart, wrestler and promoter, came in with some Big Time Wrestling stars. Gene Kiniski, Killer Kowalski, and Mighty Ursus were a new breed of athlete—sports entertainers. Stu made straight for the kitchen and put a bear hug around Gene. When the cook caught his breath, they chatted about cars, their mutual passion. Stu drove Cadillacs, buying a new one every year when the shocks gave out from hauling his stars around the western Canada wrestling circuit. "Stu, one day I'm going to own a Cadillac. That's when I'll be as successful as you!" By now, Gene knew the preferences of most of the wrestlers, including the fact that Killer, a vegetarian, would eat spaghetti with a little garlic, olive oil, and cheese. He served their food on platters, not plates.

The jingling of the phone sounded through the music and chatter of the dining room. Martha didn't speak Italian, so when Gene's Italian friends and newly arrived acquaintances called, she had to interrupt his cooking. But he didn't mind—he was pleased that they liked his food. "Yes, come. How many? Good, you have a ride? Come to the kitchen."

"Nick Caracciolo will be here soon," Gene advised.

"If I can't find room in the dining room, he can sit at the family table," my mother responded.

Gene sent pan-fried chicken and veal Milanese to the Belzberg table and instructed a waitress, "Take this linguine and the veal scaloppine to Sugarfoot. If he isn't at his table, find him and tell him his dinner's ready."

When Nick and a friend arrived at the back door, my father was surprised that they had come in a taxi. "Scotty brought us in his car," Nick explained.

"Good. Invite him in." Gene introduced them to his kitchen assistants, Mary and Salina. "These boys are from Italy," explained my father. "They've only been in Calgary for a few months." Then, placing a hand on Nick's shoulder, my father said, "How about some spaghetti and meatballs?"

My mother reported to the kitchen, "Harold Riley's just come in with a judge and a few lawyers. I'm giving them the last free table."

"I'm still hungry, Gene," said Sugarfoot, returning to the kitchen with his empty plate.

"That's easy to fix." The cook smiled, putting some pan-fried chicken on the plate.

"You know why I call you the people's chef? Because people come here to be with you. This is a classy place. I mean, no one gets out of line. Well, maybe the occasional wrestler," laughed Sugarfoot.

Around 1:00 AM, my father took off his apron. He was pleased that the crowds continued to grow every week and made a note to place a larger meat order for next Saturday night. Now he could relax and let down what little hair he had. He sauntered into the dining room and sat with the Mikkelson party for a drink.

By 3:00 AM, the tables began to empty. "Martha, could we please have some breadsticks to take home to the children. We put them in their cribs to buy a few more minutes of sleep," Barb Bishop asked. Six paper bags left with the Rowe party.

The staff cleaned up and Stella called for a couple of taxis to take them home. Mother waved goodbye and locked the kitchen door. By 4:00 AM, everyone had left, and another Saturday night at La Villa was a memory. The stairway leading to the family living quarters was so narrow that it could accommodate only one person at a time, and even then one had to turn sideways to manoeuvre around a ninety-degree twist partway up. Mother waited at the bottom step for Father to lock the front door and turn off the neon sign. He kissed the back of her neck, put his arms around her waist, and they ascended the narrow stairs together.

|Two|

THE ROMANS and my father adored Fortuna, the fickle goddess who dispensed fortune, even though, in my father's case, it was more bad luck than good. But he couldn't know that, nor would he have accepted it. He possessed a hunger for life and confidence that he could master his fate. Gene was seduced by the drama of Fortuna, as were composers such as Leoncavallo, who wrote his favourite opera, *I Pagliacci*. Canio the clown singing "Vesti la giubba" caused my father's throat to tighten and pulled the tears from his eyes. Like many immigrants, Genesio Cioni took Fortuna's lesson to heart:

> Laugh loud, Pagliaccio, forget all of your troubles,
> Laugh off the pain that so empoisons your heart …
> And yet, chin up, you'll try harder!

Fortuna worked hard in Antrodoco, a town of five thousand nestled at the foot of the Sabine Mountains. It was here that my grandfather, Sabato Cioni, the shoemaker, toiled seven days a week in a small, sweltering workshop, choking on air heavy with chemicals leached from the tanned skins. He had little time for the joys of youth and so considered himself very fortunate to have married Villemina Cattani, a gentle woman from a good family that bred priests, and to have three children: Gisetta, Giuseppe, and Gabriele. On many nights, Sabato lay gasping, his lungs panicking for air. He accepted that his life might be short, but, surprisingly, Villemina's was shorter.

The shock and sorrow hit hard, then Sabato realized that he needed another wife. What are the odds of a second happy marriage? he wondered. Fortuna liked his audacity. Just a few houses away, on Via Cutilia, lived Flavia Cardellini, twenty-five and single. There is an old Italian saying that "a twenty-six-year-old woman is like last year's wine, sour as vinegar," but Flavia was still sweet. Sweet and strong-willed, she wanted love, which was why Fortuna brought Sabato to her doorstep. They married in July 1903 and settled into family life, adding two more children—my father, Genesio, born in April 1907, and a year later, another son, Sabatino.

Shortly after my father's birth, Sabato was fortunate to earn a government job that bestowed a healthier environment, a uniform, and extra lire. He became a mailman. "Be careful when Fortuna smiles too much," Italians say. Sabato died at home in October 1908, leaving his thirty-year-old wife with five children, two of them babies.

The Cioni and Cardellini families gave what food and support they could. If only Sabato had held the government job longer, there would have been a little pension. Instead, Flavia worked in the fields, a sight that would have made Sabato's eyes implode. The only daughter, Gisa, or Gisetta as she was called, now fifteen, looked after her four younger brothers and kept house. She was lovely and a hard worker, attributes that attracted suitors. When she turned eighteen, the families arranged that she would marry Ricardo Santopinto, a *paesano* who had been working in Canada for two years. Although Flavia would be losing a helper, the two older boys were now working in the fields, and there would be one less mouth to feed.

Like many men from Antrodoco and other parts of Italy, Ricardo had responded to the Canadian Pacific Railway advertisements to come and build the railway. From the 1880s, a steady stream of men had left to earn minimal salaries that, nonetheless, were unimaginable at home. It wasn't surprising that once the railway was finished, many decided to stay. They sent back to their villages for families and brides-to-be until, by 1911, there were 114 Italians living in a Calgary community called Riverside. In 1912, Gisetta left Antrodoco to marry a man whom she had never met. Meanwhile, the older Cioni boys worked harder as times worsened, and in 1915, when Italy entered World War I, Giuseppe and Gabriele Cioni joined the Italian army to fight in the Yugoslavian campaign.

With the older children gone and the war sucking up any surplus food and clothing, Flavia's life with her two young boys was basic survival. Her one bright spot was reading Gisetta's letters. Sweet Gisetta, now and then sending tiny bits of money; brave Gisetta, telling stories about her daily routine, the city, and the Italian community helping one another—in short, about struggling to build a Canadian life with a decent man. Her words caused Flavia to think that perhaps if her young family was in Calgary, a metropolis of nearly fifty thousand, they would have a life free of war and, most important, a future. She exchanged Gisetta's news with her neighbours, many of whom also had relatives in Calgary—Serani, Fabi, Ciuffa, Grassi, Poscente, Carloni, and Corradetti.

Annibale Corradetti was a forty-nine-year-old widower living in Calgary but originally from Antrodoco. He learned of Flavia's availability from his relatives. Fortuna suggested that a woman who had struggled for seven years on her own might be willing to take the chance to come to Calgary and look after his two boys. Annibale Corradetti sent an offer of marriage to my grandmother, Flavia Cioni.

By now Flavia, thirty-seven and with two children, had slim prospects of remarrying in Antrodoco, but she was ripe for a union in Calgary. Annibale promised to pay for her passage and the wedding and to send the fare for her two young sons afterwards. She knew he owned a house with a big yard and left Italy filled with hope that she could make a new home for her young boys. She promised her sons, now aged eight and nine, that she'd see them soon. Until then, they'd be cared for by their grandmother, Rosa Cioni, and a bachelor uncle.

Annibale Corradetti was a rough and penny-pinching man. He was one of the city labourers who installed the railway ties on 8th Avenue in Calgary so that the horse-drawn wagons wouldn't bog down in the muddy roads. In later years, Fortuna laughed as he was also part of the crew that ripped out those same ties to lay asphalt for automobile traffic. If it had been allowed, he would have taken the wooden ties home, for Annibale was a man who scrounged for every free scrap he could find. He didn't pay for anything if he could help it. He even played an accordion with a broken base, preferring to inflict agony on himself and any listeners rather than paying to fix it.

What Annibale lacked in generosity, he made up for in drive. He didn't think about Fortuna, he thought about how he could make an extra penny. It was his custom to go to the Bow River as the ice started to break and snag floating logs with a grappling hook. With formidable strength, Annibale piled them on his cart and pushed the load a mile uphill. After cutting the logs into planks, he built his own house and dug a large garden. In summer and fall, he took garlic and other produce to vendors in the City Hall Market to barter for chickens, then he built a chicken coop in his yard and collected the eggs.

Over the years, he salvaged enough wood to build nine shacks, which he rented out. He looked forward to his monthly rounds to collect rent. Tenants soon learned that if they couldn't meet their obligations, the landlord applied his own remedy. In knee-high snow and temperatures that froze water pipes and windows, Annibale pulled the door off the hinges of a defaulter's house until the rent was in his grasp.

As soon as Flavia arrived in Calgary, she became Annibale's wife and mother to his two sons. In 1918, when she gave birth to another son, Nick, she realized that Annibale's priorities were his own family, not her sons in Italy. She knew that it would be up to her to find the money to bring Genesio and Sabatino to Calgary. If she took in laundry or a boarder, as some women did, Annibale would take the extra cash for himself. The same thing would happen if she sold eggs or vegetables from the garden. The only way to get the passage money was without his knowledge, and secrets were dangerous. He would beat her if he found out and, worse, confiscate the money.

Fortuna guided my grandmother to the Roma Grocery, a few blocks from home. Dominic Gasberri had opened the little store when his family arrived in Calgary in 1909. The Roma Grocery catered to the tastes of the small Italian community, selling food in bulk so that minimal amounts could be purchased when money was tight. There were salami and prosciutto hanging over barrels of olives, a large container of olive oil with a spigot to fill vessels with the liquid gold, and mouthwatering cheeses—mild, blue, and hard—challenging the aroma of dark-roasted coffee.

My grandmother sought the assistance of another Flavia, the owner's daughter, Flavia Gasberri. Their scheme was simple. Miss Gasberri padded the bill, charging for items that weren't taken and increasing some unit costs by a few pennies. At the end of the month, Annibale went to settle, eyeing each item before paying forty dollars for a bill that might have cost only thirty-five. The next day my grandmother collected the five dollars from her confidante, and the monthly cycle began again.

In summer, Annibale's 220-foot lot overflowed with vegetables. My grandmother risked selling small amounts of his produce to Roma Grocery. She didn't do this often for she knew that her husband had memorized the number of garlic shoots and the length of the green beans that he tended daily.

Where could she keep the extra money? It was too dangerous to hide it at home; Annibale might come across it. Gisetta, her stepdaughter, became her ally in the scheme, keeping the money at her house. Each month Flavia's nerves knotted as Annibale went to pay the Roma bill. When he returned unalarmed, she counted her blessings and began to plan for next month's purchases. She had three more children in three years.

After saving for three years, there was only $100—not even half of the $250 needed for one ticket to Calgary and a little food money. She must try to save more, maybe $10 each month. Genesio was now in grade four, and his letters to her were growing shorter. It was what he didn't say that hurt her. He had stopped asking when he and his brother would come to Calgary.

"Take courage," whispered Fortuna. So my grandmother persevered. Three more years passed before she had saved enough for one ticket to Calgary. She decided to send for Genesio. She rationalized that her older son could start working sooner and help to raise the money to bring his younger brother.

Flavia had been scared to tell Annibale about Genesio's impending arrival until she realized that her secret was now irrelevant. She simply said, "Genesio is coming to Calgary. I sent money for a ticket." She watched the black eyebrows raise and the powerful jaw drop. Annibale swung his arm out and then let it fall. She thought she saw a momentary smirk of admiration.

In April 1923, my father, accompanied by his uncle, left Antrodoco for the provincial capital of Riete. For Genesio, Uncle bought a one-way steamship ticket to New York for $150 and with another $50 purchased a single rail passage from New York City to Calgary. He also bought them train tickets to Naples and slipped the remainder of Flavia's money into his inner jacket pocket. They boarded a train south to Rome and then on to the port of Naples.

Genesio's Grade Four class in Antrodoco, 1919. He is standing in the back row on the far right. Inspector Fenelli and Teacher Tetti are seated in the first row. (Photo courtesy of Ezio Carloni, Antrodoco.)

Naples was a different land, its sights, colours, sounds, and smells tingling their senses. Uncle bought some mozzarella cheese, red wine, and bread baked with tomatoes and olive oil—a local specialty called pizza. Tired, the travellers stopped at a little piazza and set out the modest feast on the edge of a fountain. It was their last meal together, and Genesio nervously spilled some wine as Uncle toasted *un buon viaggio*, a smooth voyage. They moved along the dock, searching for the Lloyd Sabaudo Line. When they found the departure area, Uncle took out the remaining money from his jacket pocket and, removing my father's cap, carefully pinned it inside. "This will buy your food," he said. Then Uncle enveloped him, knowing that it might be the last time they would ever hold each other. "Six thousand miles away, your mother is waiting for you," he whispered and nudged his nephew into line.

The teenager joined the human ribbon passing from one official's hand to another. He mimicked those ahead, showing his ticket and answering the twenty-nine perfunctory questions: he was single, he had $50 cash, he was a farmer, and he was going to Calgary to his mother's house. Suddenly, a white coat snapped him to attention and a doctor began prying his eyes open, sticking fingers in his mouth, thumping his bony chest, rolling a fist down his spine, and poking his joints. "Move along, move along," they were told.

Genesio lugged his suitcase up the steep gangplank of the *Conte Rosso*, glimpsing the opulent wood carving and twinkling mirrors in the first-class dining room as he descended into growing darkness. More than 2,300 Italians were sailing to America that day; 1,889 were my father's companions in third class.

Genesio turned sixteen during the voyage, but there was no one to wish him a happy birthday. Genesio felt old. He'd watched over Sabatino, comforting him when he cried for their mother. Each day his heart had grown heavier waiting for word from his mother that they could join her in Calgary.

The day Uncle had shown him the money that his mother had sent, Genesio was a child again. He danced for joy with Sabatino. Then, more news from Uncle, there was only enough money for one fare. The brothers cried like babies. At first, Genesio didn't want to go, but Uncle explained that their mother had saved the money to send for him, and once he was in Calgary, they would work together to bring Sabatino. Knowing this didn't stop the sadness from creeping into the Cioni house, it didn't stop the apprehension from building.

Genesio memorized the faces, the voices, the stories, the touches, and the

The *Conte Rosso*, the ship that brought Genesio to New York in 1923.

smells of those he loved, and the details of his town: the houses shoulder to shoulder on his street, the nervous chickens squawking in the market, the heat from the communal baking oven, the hundreds of steps to the Madonna of the Grotto, and the openness of the Piazza del Popolo. He often joined the old men who gathered daily in the piazza, feeling he was one of them. Around and around the piazza they'd stroll, Genesio memorizing the shapes and colours of the stones. In years to come, he wanted to be able to close his eyes and return to his town.

On the dreaded day of departure, Genesio pressed his lips against Nonna Rosa's wrinkled cheek and kept walking as she crumpled into Sabatino's arms. Earlier, Genesio had said goodbye to Sabatino. They spoke about being reunited in Calgary, about being brave while waiting for Sabatino's turn. Genesio vowed that, with Fortuna, he would work hard to make that time short for his brother.

During the train journey from New York, Genesio thought of all the things his mother had written about this place called Calgary. He was anxious to see the Rocky Mountains that she called giants. She had described the wooden houses in Riverside, noting that there were spaces between each one the width of the Velino River. There were large fields the size of the piazza covered with grass, and snow in winter. Flavia had told him that she felt free under the high blue skies and could see the mountains more than fifty miles away. She had told him that she had learned some English, but having never heard English until the previous week in New York, Genesio hadn't appreciated the achievement. What he thought the most odd were her stories about people of different nationalities—Ukrainians, Irish, and Germans—living next door to Italians in Riverside, while on the other side of the river were the English.

On 23 May 1923, twenty-eight days after leaving the lights of Naples, Genesio stood on the concrete platform of the Calgary train station. Part of him was yearning for his old family in Antrodoco while he tried to control the anxiety and excitement of seeing his mother and his new family in Calgary. He didn't know just how fortunate he was to be there, part of the last flow of immigrants who arrived just as the Italian and Canadian governments were turning off the tap. Mussolini was encouraging Italians to seek better opportunities inside their country; restricting their ability to leave helped his cause. The Canadian government continued making regulations to favour immigrants from the United Kingdom, Holland, and northern Europe. Italians were not wanted.

Genesio becomes a barber. The graduating class of Hemphill Barber College, December 1925. Genesio is seated in the first row on the far left.

Genesio stood in the train station, uncertain of his next step, but then Fortuna intervened in the person of Sam Ross. Sam was cutting through the train station when he spied Genesio. Sam, an Italian, had lived in Canada for ten years; he'd anglicized his name and applied his natural talent to playing cards and betting. The professional gambler was adept at reading body language. Seeing the disoriented young man in the station, he asked in Italian, "*Sta Italiano?* You're Italian, aren't you? You need help? Where are you going?"

Hearing the familiar language jolted Genesio into action. He pointed to the address on a folded letter held tightly in his hand. "Do you have money for a taxi?" Sam asked and watched Genesio take off his cap and fumble with the lining. "Never mind. Come with me." Sam put him in a taxi and paid the driver. "Don't worry that no one's here to meet you. Your mother probably didn't know when you'd arrive. By the way, kid, my best friend lives across the street from your mother. I guess we'll be seeing each other."

Flavia heard a timid knock on the door. Instantly, she thought of Genesio, and when she opened the door, there he was. She held him close as if she'd never let him go. The bony young man was double the size of the boy she had left behind. He was as tall as his father and, when she let him go, she saw the same steady, loving gaze.

To Annibale, my father looked like an able-bodied person who could contribute to the family. The sooner the new arrival signed up to work for the city or the railway, the better. Relatives would put in a good word with co-workers, and in a couple of days Flavia's son would be bringing money home to pay for his room and board.

"Genesio will learn English," Flavia said. "He'll go to barber's school."

"I'm not paying for any damn school. He's sixteen and he'll work."

"I have money to pay for it," Flavia struck back.

She stood firm on these plans, partly to make amends for the years of separation, but also because she wanted a better life for her son. Genesio had no interest in barbering, but for her sake, he would get used to the idea.

Like his father, Genesio began his career working with shoes; he got a job at the Calgary Shoe Hospital, downtown on 8th Avenue and 1st Street. He learned English by listening and talking to the businessmen as he shined their shoes. To appease his stepfather, Genesio paid rent.

Two years after my father had arrived in Calgary, he could speak English well enough to enrol in the barber course at the Hemphill Barber College, adjacent to the Hemphill Automobile Gas Tractor School. My father liked working with the elegant pearl-handled, natural-bristle shaving brushes and chatting with customers, but he had little interest in hair that wasn't his own. Nevertheless, as a student he learned the basics by practising on people willing to get a bargain haircut for fifteen cents and a shave for ten cents. After six months, he graduated just before Christmas in 1925. Flavia beamed all through the celebratory dinner she had prepared. Lately though, her stomach had been bothering her with stabbing pains that came in waves. If only it didn't hurt so much, the evening would have been perfect.

After graduation, my father found a barbering job with the help of Sam Ross, who seemed to know everyone. Flavia cried when her son gave her his first paycheque. Now they would save to bring Sabatino to Calgary. Meanwhile, Flavia's attacks were becoming so frequent that she could no longer hide them. My father was with her when she collapsed. "You need a doctor!" he shouted nervously, gathering her into his arms. But the pain passed and she promised that she would ask Annibale to take her for a checkup.

When Flavia told her husband about the pains, he shrugged it off, saying she should get the kids to do more work. Fearful of doctors, she didn't insist, but then she had another attack that was so bad it scared even Annibale. He ran to his cousin next door, who called an ambulance. Flavia was rushed to the General Hospital, the two Corradetti men carrying her. She died of a ruptured gall bladder on 17 February 1926, at the age of forty-nine. Annibale told Genesio and the other children that their mother had died, adding that he couldn't afford a marker for her grave.

Genesio wept when he thought of the seven years he and Sabatino had waited in Italy while their mother had struggled to reunite them. He wrote to Sabatino to share their tragedy, feeling guilty but also glad that he had been able to spend three more years with their mother. Waves of sorrow washed over Genesio. He hated the way Annibale had dismissed Flavia, yelling and swearing at her and the children, and burying her without a sign of gratitude. He packed his bags, vowing to create a life that would make his mother proud. The first thing on his list was to earn enough money to bring Sabatino to Calgary.

|Three|

LA VIA

THE STABILITY OF
THE FAMILY HOME
LAY BEHIND EVERYTHING.

—Ignazio Silone,
The Seed Beneath the Snow,
in *The Abruzzo Trilogy*

MY FATHER was fortunate that his older half-sister, Gisetta, her husband, Ricardo Santopinto, and their five children lived on 4th Avenue, a couple of blocks from Annibale. The siblings had different mothers, but both had inherited their father's kind disposition. Gisetta was thirteen years his senior, and Genesio, mourning Flavia's death, welcomed a second mother.

Gisetta understood the loneliness of being an orphan, the panic of being left alone in a world where you are a newcomer. It was then, at the age of nineteen, that Genesio really became a man. Gisetta reclaimed their history with stories about their father, about how Sabato had worked so hard trying to better himself to make an easier life for the two women whom he had married. "I hope that I'm like our father," Genesio told her.

Gisetta spent much of her time in the kitchen, and as the siblings talked, Genesio found himself taking an interest in her cooking. She was an alchemist, transforming the most meagre ingredients into delicious meals. She produced plate-licking sauce from sparerib bones, browning them in olive oil with a little garlic, onions, salt, and herbs and then adding tomatoes to simmer.

One day as Gisetta was washing a sink full of potatoes Genesio asked, "Teach me to make gnocchi." She laughed, thinking it was another of his jokes, until she saw the seriousness in his eyes. "Okay. Do you want to write down the recipe?"

"No. I'll remember it."

"It's important to start with old potatoes," she began. "They're dry and won't absorb too much flour. That means the gnocchi will be light. Boil the potatoes, peel them, and push them through the ricer." She pointed to the old aluminum contraption with long, red handles. She filled the strainer basket with cooled potatoes, positioned the plunger on top, and pushed the long, red handles together. Thin strands of starch wiggled through the basket holes onto the wooden board that Ricardo had made for mixing dough. "Add an egg, a sprinkle of salt, and enough flour to make dough that's elastic but not sticky." She watched her brother's hands feel the dough, surprised that he was able to produce the right consistency. "Very good." She patted his shoulder. "We'll let it rest awhile."

"You rest, too," Genesio said. "I'm going to play soccer with my nephews. Call me when it's time to finish the job."

Gisetta's boys pleaded with their uncle to play longer. "I have something important to do," he laughed as he kicked the ball over the fence into Mrs. Buccini's yard.

"Cut pieces of dough and roll them like long cigars," Gisetta directed, again surprised by the quickness of her brother's hands. "Good. Now cut half-inch pieces. I'll get my old fork." She brought out one with long tines and threw some flour over it. "Roll

Gisa (Gisetta) Cioni Santopinto, Gene's sister, cooking at home, 1929.

Gisetta's Gnocchi

(Serves 3)

1 lb. old or baking potatoes

6 oz. flour

½ tsp. salt

1 egg

Boil potatoes and put them through a ricer. Add the remaining ingredients, mix thoroughly, and turn out on a floured board. Roll into 1-in. finger shapes, then cut into ½-in. lengths. Roll each piece over the back of the tines of a fork to make ridges.

Place a few pieces at a time in boiling salted water, removing them when they float to the top. Put cooked gnocchi in a serving dish with some sauce and continue until all are done. Sprinkle with grated cheese and serve immediately.

For 6 servings: Use 2 eggs and triple the other ingredients. For 8 servings: Use 4 lb. potatoes, 4 c. flour, 1 tsp. salt, and 4 eggs.

a piece of dough across the back of the tines to make ridges. This'll hold the sauce." She demonstrated and watched her brother do the rest.

At dinner that evening, she asked her family, "How are the gnocchi?"

"Your best yet."

Genesio was restless. He decided to leave town for awhile to get away from the sad memories and to avoid seeing Annibale. He found a barbering job in Jasper and stayed there for several months, until he realized that Flavia's premature death had released him from his obligation to be a barber. Genesio's best friend was a cousin named Mario Grassi, a waiter in the dining room at the Palliser Hotel. One gnocchi dinner convinced Mario that Genesio had talent, and he helped him get a job as a busboy at the hotel.

Many *paesani* from Antrodoco worked in the Palliser dining room. Two of the best waiters at the time were Mario and Marino Manzara. Genesio watched their style and grace as they effortlessly carried the large stainless steel trays, firmly anchored on their shoulders. In one smooth motion, they set the plate before the customer, removing the steel dome at a slight angle to reveal a steaming dinner. They were attentive but never intrusive. Customers asked to be seated in their service areas. He saw how naturally they chatted with patrons. Even when they had to run the long halls between the kitchen, the dining room, and the suites of the "Paralyser," as the employees called it, they were always calm and in control.

The plum summertime jobs for young people were at the CPR hotels in the mountains. The scenery and the tips couldn't be beat. Gisetta's eldest daughter, Jean, and a group of her eighteen-year-old friends applied for summer employment as chambermaids and helpers in the dining room at the Banff Springs Hotel and the Chateau Lake Louise. My father loved the mountains and leaped at the opportunity to spend a few summers at each of the hotel dining rooms, first as a busboy and then as a waiter.

Wealthy American and Canadian families flocked to the Rockies, and the hotels were always jammed. Since tables in the dining room were in high demand, the dishes had to be cleared and reset quickly. Genesio picked up the pace; he was always on the run.

As a welcome respite, my father and his friends would bicycle to a nearby lake to swim, and often he surprised them with a picnic. Eating outside in the mountain air had been one of my father's favourite pastimes in Antrodoco. He often had asked Nonna and Uncle to take Sabatino and him for a walk in the mountains, where they would pause for a little lunch of bread and cheese as they sat overlooking the valley. At school, my father had eaten his lunch outside so that he could inhale the sweet aroma of olives and chestnuts mixed in the mountain air. In the Rockies, he filled his lungs with the crisp, pungent odour of firs and pines.

Then Fortuna smelled an opportunity for Genesio—a job vacancy for a sous-chef in the Palliser Hotel kitchen. My father learned how to prepare the basic repertoire of English food for which the CPR hotels were highly regarded: cream and French onion soups, roasted prime rib and other meats, steak and kidney pie, hollandaise and Béarnaise sauces, grilled salmon, deep-fried halibut and chips, and scalloped, mashed, or hash brown potatoes. Genesio was now a "Canadian-style" cook, but once he had mastered the basics, he was anxious to branch out.

"Fortuna helps the brave," Italians say. This was never truer than during the Depression years, when the economy was as bleak as the dry dirt on the farms, and when desperation replaced usefulness as a skill for basic survival. Genesio had stopped sending money to Sabatino. He made so little, and now that Sabatino was working in Italy, it seemed that they would be two brothers in two countries. In 1931, eight years after his arrival, my father earned a job as a cook on the work trains. There he learned to be efficient in the confines of a railway-car kitchen and to master cooking on the temperamental wood-burning stove that took up most of the space. Dressed in cook's whites, Gene, as my father was now known, managed the makeshift home on the rails, preparing meals for the bridge and road gangs who maintained train tracks and trestles in the mountains of Alberta and British Columbia.

After preparing breakfast, my father foraged for berries, mushrooms, wild garlic, and dandelions—as he had learned in the hills and forests near Antrodoco—to invigorate meals. Almost four years of this work made him restless, so in 1935 my father rode his fate to Trail, British Columbia, to visit his relatives, the Poscente family. This small smelter town, strung along the mountains, felt as familiar as Antrodoco. Italians had recreated the homes they'd left behind. Roads wound up the hillside past houses built into the earth, one above the other. On the hills, stairs ran in every direction connecting neighbours, the town centre, and the railway station.

Trail Creek meandered through the Gulch on its way to the Columbia River. On Rossland Avenue, the railway tracks ran across the front yards of the houses and Trail Creek ran across the back. Sofia and Vincenzo Poscente lived in one of these houses with their five children. The eldest son, Tony, was a close friend of my father from school days in Antrodoco.

Fortuna had brought Gene to the one town in the west that had escaped the Depression. Here, the giant CPR smelter operated around the clock, processing the lead, zinc, copper, gold, and silver needed to finance and build ships, airplanes, and communications infrastructure to strengthen the country. An army of workers mined and distilled the wealth. They lived in boarding houses and hotels. It wasn't long before my father found a job as a cook at the Montana Hotel, across the street from the Poscente home.

The three-storey Montana Hotel and beer parlour had been built by Isaac Georgetti, the first Italian immigrant in town, and was owned by the Buckna family. The hotel was home to fifty immigrant bachelors, and my father was hired to cook for the shift that worked from three in the afternoon until eleven at night. This entailed preparing midnight dinner and making lunches for work the next day. Preparations for the midnight dinner began in early evening, after the bullcook had piled logs and kindling

Gene, in his kitchen whites, takes a break on a CPR work train, 1931.

into the wood-burning stove to bring it to the right temperature. My father seasoned large pieces of meat—beef, pork, and sometimes lamb—for dinner and for sandwiches that would fill the workers the next day.

It wasn't long before Gene began to branch out, introducing a few Italian foods alongside the English fare. He flavoured lamb chops with rosemary and garlic, not mint sauce. Sometimes he cooked a side of spaghetti to replace mashed potatoes. He brushed prime rib roasts with olive oil, a little garlic, and black pepper before roasting them to a succulent medium-rare, rather than the traditional well-done. In late summer, his specialty was sautéed eggplant, tomatoes, and sage, and in winter he opened cans of stewed tomatoes, adding a little baking soda to neutralize the acidic taste and, before serving, stirring in crunched soda biscuits to give texture to a delicious side dish to accompany beef and lamb.

My father loved to watch people enjoy his food as he sat visiting with them. For him, the highlight of the evening was taking off his apron and joining the men as they ate, not to hear compliments but to listen to their stories from back home as well as the gossip from the smelter. The isolation of the kitchen and the heat of the stove were made bearable by these nightly conversations, for my father loved to talk and joke almost as much as he loved to cook. By one in the morning, the Montana was quiet. The beer parlour had closed, the men were asleep, and the kitchen staff had cleaned up and gone home.

This is when my father began to prepare lunch for the morning shift. The men looked forward to the huge sandwiches that he stuffed into their metal lunch buckets. Gene took pleasure in cutting generous pieces of roasted meats to cover the slices of warm bread he had baked. He made forty sandwiches, wrapped each in waxed paper, and put two in the bottom of each lunch bucket. Then he wedged in some fresh fruit—an apple, pear, peach, or some plums—and cookies or slivers of apple pie baked by the two Buckna sisters, who cooked during the day. Around five in the morning, other kitchen staff arrived to cook breakfast. By six, my father filled Thermoses with hot coffee, hooked them into the top half and closed the buckets. He cooked the eggs and wished the men good day. As they grabbed their lunches, he headed off to bed.

Gene spent much of his free time with Tony Poscente, and on Saturdays they dressed for a night on the town. The pair wore crisp white shirts, laundered by Sofia, tucked under dark suits and adorned with wide silk ties. My father added his grey fedora, adjusting it to his trademark angle, covering his right eye—the lazy

Gene and his friend Tony Poscente enjoy a night out in Trail, BC, c. 1935.

one that hovered. As a finale, he jabbed a diamond stick pin into his tie, just below the Windsor knot.

One Saturday night, in the autumn of 1935, they followed the smells and sounds to the annual fair, where, between the midway rides and the concessions, they came across a strange-looking booth with a curtain. Ever curious, they found a photo-machine and arranged themselves, with Tony squeezed a little in front and to the right. They put a dime in the slot and looked straight ahead, lips curled in a slight smile. Flash! Waiting as directed, they heard noise and then from a slit under a large black arrow came photos of the two young heartthrobs in control of their destiny—the Depression be damned!

Sofia's young children loved having Gene around. As they ran to greet him, he would move his hip forward to make it easier for Dante, Julio, and Eleanor's little fingers to slip inside his jacket pocket and pull out candies. On Sundays, Gene savoured the Poscente family and Aunt Sofia's cooking as he sought to fill the void left by his mother's death and the loss of his relatives in Italy. After the dinner dishes were cleared, Gene and Sofia immersed themselves in memories of Antrodoco, re-membering the food they so loved. They dissected and compared family recipes, debated which were the most important ingredients, challenged each other's notion of acceptable substitutions, discussed the "feel" and colour of food, and reminisced about stories heard at the communal oven, where news and gossip rose as the bread baked.

"I made some chicken cacciatore at the Montana. The men loved it," Gene told Sofia.

"Work in a restaurant," she responded. "You can try new dishes, create Italian and Canadian foods. Be your own boss. I think there's a job in Nelson. Our cousins there could help you."

In autumn 1936, Tony, his father, and young brother, Dante, drove Gene to Nelson. The little town was stunningly beautiful, set on the edge of Kootenay Lake and surrounded by the Selkirk Mountains. They asked for directions at the Coletti Grocery on Baker Street and then continued down Baker and around the corner to Stanley Street, where they stopped at a little eatery a few steps below the sidewalk. The Colettis and De Ferros, Poscente cousins who owned a shoe store, had roots in Antrodoco and helped my father settle in.

The job was to cook and manage the small restaurant. My father had high expectations but quickly realized that there was a demand for only breakfast and lunch for the transient workers from the nearby logging and mining camps and for employees from the railway, the lake ferries, and the government administrative offices. The workers ate dinner with their families, in the camps, or at boarding houses; there was no dinner clientele in this small town, no customers to dine on the creative foods that my father wanted to prepare. After a few months, he grew restless again.

"Who changes his conditions, changes his fortune," Gene muttered the Italian proverb as he boarded the train for Vancouver in 1937 to look for work. Vancouver, a city of nearly three hundred thousand, presented opportunity. The Italian population alone was more than three thousand. Gene had heard of Achilles Pini, one of the seven brothers of a restaurant family that owned two Italian restaurants: the Paris Inn on Seymour and the Lido on Main Street, which also had housed Pini's nightclub in the basement. The nightclub had been a dine and dance run by Tony Pini, a nephew. Gene sought out the Lido restaurant, where he met Achilles and his wife. Both families had roots in the Abruzzo region. They talked and ate. My father thought that he might get a job there until he learned that times were so tough that Tony Pini and his family had gone up north to mine for a living.

Gene knew that sometimes you had to make your own good fortune. Knowing that business was just getting by, he mustered the courage and said, "Achilles, I want to offer my services to you free of charge. I'll do anything. Wash dishes, prepare food, cook. Just let me learn how you manage the restaurant. And, oh, give me my meals."

The young man's openness, warmth, and intensity impressed Achilles. "Let's see what you can do. We'll try it for a week."

Gene stayed for almost a year, weathering the worst of the Depression in the Italian restaurant and finding comfort within the extended Pini family, their friends, and the large Italian community. He went shopping for restaurant supplies at Peter Tosi's large import business, where he bought olive oil from California, Genoa salami from Piedmont, and Romano and Parmesan cheeses from Italy. He got his hair cut at Alberto Principi's shop, where the two exchanged barber stories and Alberto found a sympathetic ear in which to confide his secret passion for food and desire to be in the restaurant business.

My father learned from the Pinis how the family worked together and shared responsibilities, when and from whom to order food supplies, the reasoning behind the menu choices, the minimum number of staff needed to run a dining room and nightclub, and the profit margins. He considered staying in Vancouver, but he was homesick for Calgary and his own family. In 1938, after being away for three years, Gene returned home, anxious to apply his entrepreneurial knowledge and experience and eager to see his family and friends again. He was thirty-one years old.

Gisetta cried with joy when she saw Gene. He was slimmer and more confident, and he talked incessantly about cooking. He was full of plans to get a job where he could determine the menu and prepare the foods his way, applying Italian culinary techniques to English food. They talked about the fact that Sabatino had married and now had a young son and how Sabatino was making a life for his family in Rome. Gisetta lamented that her fifteen-year-old son, Nino, was in a group of neighbourhood youths who pulled pranks such as ringing doorbells and scurrying away, picking pennies out of the milk chutes, and helping themselves to abundant gardens. Magi, her older son, had caught some of them and warned them to behave.

Over lunch, she gave the latest Riverside news, telling how Magi, who worked after school in Louis Carloni's Canadian Shoe Shine store downtown, had escaped the police raids aimed at finding gambling in the back room. Gambling—slots and cards—was still a favourite although illegal pastime among many men in the community. The community loved horse races, and betting at the track was legal. Sometimes on weekends Alex Aquilini, Dante Signori, and others still took their working horses out for an impromptu race along the banks of the Bow River. My father, his friends, and the neighbourhood loved these events. After they cleaned up the lunch dishes together, Gisetta offered a room in the basement; Genesio was home again.

Gene's next stop was to visit the home of Sam Ross, where Fortuna lay in wait.

My father and Sam Ross had become good friends since the day Sam had found him at the Calgary train station. Sam and his wife, Goldie, had treated my father as one of their family. Sam had advised "the kid," as he called my father, on how to succeed as an immigrant: develop a skill and be very good at it; if you like to cook, be the best. A prosperous image was important, too. My father already believed in *la bella figura*, and looking good had become his style.

When the Rosses were expecting their second baby, in 1926, Goldie had written to her younger sister, Martha, to come to Calgary to help out. She was living on a farm in North Dakota with their father, four younger siblings, and a stepmother, with her own two children, when the letter arrived from Calgary. Goldie's invitation and money were the sixteen-year-old's ticket out. She was on the next train. But Calgary wasn't quite what Martha expected. Goldie, six years older, and Sam had a busy lifestyle that was alien to the small-town sister. Calgary was bigger than she could ever have imagined, and even though she had hated being on the farm, she became so desperately homesick that she would go around singing, "The biscuits are tough and I can't get enough, there's no place like home."

That day in 1936, it was Martha who opened the Rosses' door when my father knocked. "Gene, you're back!" Her American twang snapped in his ears. She gave him a spontaneous hug. Taking off his fedora, he noticed her cornflower blue eyes dance with interest as he laid a friendly kiss on her cheek. The woman before him bore little resemblance to the shy, gawky teenager he had encountered twelve years earlier. He had heard that she was working as a waitress and then cashier in Jimmy Condon's new café, the Palace of Eats, downtown near the Hudson's Bay store.

My stylish mother beside the Empress Theatre in Calgary, 1926.

Gene and Martha's wedding photo taken by Reno Corradetti, 28 June 1939.

Hoping to encourage romance, at dinner Sam told Gene the story of how he had met Goldie. "It was Fortuna," he began. "One Sunday, I was driving through Bowness Park and I spotted this gorgeous woman. She had golden hair and she was riding a horse. I put my foot on the gas to get closer but the car backfired. The horse reared and threw the beauty to the ground. I jumped out of the car and grabbed the horse's bridle so he wouldn't trample her. Then I helped her up. After tying her horse to the bumper, we drove back to her residence and got a doctor. Thankfully, she was okay. The next Sunday I went back to the park looking for her. I drove around for so long that I ran out of gas. I was halfway up a hill. The car began rolling backwards. I put on the hand brake and got out, but the car rolled and pinned me against a tree. Just then, Goldie rode by. She saw me squashed like an ant. She got help. My knee was busted and I was laid up for a couple weeks. As soon as I could, I went back to the park. I found her and proposed on the spot."

Goldie interjected, "I said yes, but only if my diamond ring was bigger than his."

Martha and Gene dated for a few months, and there was no doubt that she liked her Italian suitor. He was fun and loved to tease her. "I'm going to call you Marta. It's how we say your name in Italian. Such a beautiful woman deserves a pretty name." He was always asking her opinion until he realized that she didn't need any encouragement to speak her mind. Gene was well-dressed, as was she, and he took her to concerts, to visit friends, and sometimes out for dinner. He had good manners and a respectful regard that made her feel comfortable, but although she enjoyed his company, commitment was not part of her history. She had become adept at declining proposals of marriage from successful immigrants and entrepreneurs.

Martha did trust Gene enough, though, to tell him the story of her childhood in North Dakota. She told him about her German parents leaving their small acreage in Romania at the turn of the twentieth century to farm on the American prairies. She was the seventh of eleven children; Goldie was the third. Her parents had a happy marriage and with hard work did well enough to buy a decent-sized farm, which enabled them to feed and clothe their brood. At fifteen, Goldie left to go to Calgary with her older brother, Manuel, to find a job. When her mother died at the age of thirty-seven, Martha, the eldest girl still at home, had to quit school in grade eight and tend her four younger siblings. She adored her father and worked hard to bring order to the family. Her father soon remarried, but "the old hag" was a hateful woman who locked the pantry, giving food only to her own children. Worse still, Martha's father had chosen to support his wife, believing her stories rather than his children's truths; it poisoned his relationship with Martha. Then, escaping to Calgary, Martha thought that she would find serenity in her sister's house but even there Sam and Goldie's volatile personalities sparked many marital arguments.

When my father returned to Calgary, Sam helped him get a job at a gambling and bootlegging joint. Each day, he climbed the stairs to a door with a peephole, giving a signal to the guard at the door and then made his way to the kitchen to prepare food for hungry gamblers. It was temporary employment until another opportunity arose. Fortuna teased with an offer to work outside Calgary. Gene went straight to Martha and proposed.

Without hesitation she said, "No."

"Stay, Gene, don't run," Fortuna whispered. Recovering somewhat, he asked, "Marta, what are you waiting for? Prince Charming?" She raised her left brow at his impertinence, but he continued. "You're twenty-nine. You're not getting any younger and you won't find anyone better than me. I love you! Marta, please marry me."

"I'll think about it," she finally agreed. Gene's words rolled through her mind. She thought him kind and full of ideas. He was not afraid to work hard. Most important of all, he valued her opinions, he saw her as his equal, his partner; whatever they did, they would do it together and for that she truly loved him.

"Trust me. I'm the right man at the right time," he joked.

My parents were married on 28 June 1939. Since my mother was Lutheran, they were not allowed to marry within Our Lady of Perpetual Help Church. However, because she agreed to bring up any children as Catholic, they were able to exchange vows in the church rectory. The bride was beaming in her navy georgette dress with matching bowler hat, while the thirty-two-year-old groom was sedate in an ink blue suit and striped, navy and white silk tie. On their way to the reception at Gisetta's home, my father said to his bride, "I'm the most fortunate man alive." It wasn't long before my mother conceded, "Marriage is the happiest time of my life."

Fortuna had settled Gene and his brother, Sabatino, with different lives in different countries, but pleased them with supportive, loving wives. Yet, although their letters to each other were filled with information, there was no mention of feelings. It had been sixteen years since they had shared their hopes and made promises, not knowing that Fortuna had other plans. They knew that expressing their emotions would have to wait until they met again; for now, the latest news would suffice.

|Four|

GENESIO VINCENZO GALDINO CIONI was my father's name in its full glory. It paid homage to his ancestors and to their cultural roots in Antrodoco, a town begun when Etruscan invaders decided to stay. The name "Genesio" connected to the Romans, who had established the town's historical significance. Then it was called *Interocrea*, "between places," positioned at the junction where the *Via Salaria*, the main salt-trading road north from Rome, branched in two directions. The name predicted my father's future.

"Vincenzo" recalled deceased relatives, and "Galdino" was bestowed to celebrate the saint's day on which my father was born. During the schism following the death of Pope Adrian IV in 1159, Saint Galdino, the bishop of Milan, had remained loyal to Roman candidate Pope Alexander III rather than to the Holy Roman Emperor, Barbarossa's choice. Years later, as papal legate, Galdino rid the province of opposing priests and consecrated new bishops loyal to Rome. Celebrating the saint's day and my father's birthday on 18 April was a family tradition. It reminded them of the special relationship between their town and Rome.

The family name, "Cioni," was not a common one. A loose translation is "of Giovanni." Cioni heraldry notes the family origins in Florence in the fourteenth century, and during that period a Cioni created one of the gold panels of the Duomo baptistery door. No one knows precisely how the name spread southward to Abruzzo, but in the small town of Antrodoco in the nineteenth century, there were a couple of families

∽ **WHAT'S** ⬠
IN A NAME?

WORDS ARE ONE THING AND
DEEDS ARE ANOTHER.

—Ignazio Silone, *Fontamara*,
in *The Abruzzo Trilogy*

named Cioni, distant cousins perhaps, whose lineage and relationship were lost in memory.

Surprisingly, Antrodoco returned from obscurity in the nineteenth and twentieth centuries. Because the town was situated in the geographic centre of the Italian boot, the nearby canyons seemed a significant place for Garibaldi to begin the struggle to unify the provinces of Italy. But the creation of Italy did little for Antrodoco except to take its men to fight wars. On 12 October 1924, Mussolini drove through town in a two-seater roadster, his goggles pushed back over the top of his brown leather helmet so that the hundreds of people crowding the Piazza del Popolo could get a better look. He liked this mountain area and, learning of the town's bull's-eye position in Italy, later established a hideaway in the nearby mountains.

But being appreciated and remembered is not always good. When Mussolini redrew the provincial boundaries in 1927, Antrodoco became part of Lazio, the seat of Il Duce in Rome. The locals and the emigrants from Antrodoco resisted in the only way they could, by clinging passionately to their Abruzzese traditions through their names and their foods.

Genesio Cioni was bewildered but also excited by the Calgary that he found when he arrived in 1923. He stood on downtown streets covered in railway ties, hearing the sounds of life in English and smelling roast beef and boiled vegetables. He took refuge in Riverside with the small Italian community that now housed more than four hundred people. Settled here, he began to look around at a very different place. Through his mother and older half-sister, Gisetta, and in the comfort of a dialect inflected with Latin, Genesio connected with the eighty other Antrodocani in the community. These were his *paesani*, formed by the same land, history, and customs. Next to blood relations, they were the people he could trust, people who would give him unconditional support.

Paesani knew one another by their nicknames. The meaning could be historical, descriptive, physical, or sometimes ironic, but subtlety was never a concern. Names such as "*mezzo metro*" ("half metre") could apply to height and other body parts. "Folded ear," "crazy," "virile," "grape crusher": these names were worn as a personal coat of arms. Genesio's family nickname was "*pellaru*," literally "the person who works with animal skins." The name linked him to his father, the shoemaker, and to generations before him.

Although he spoke mostly in dialect, my father had learned

the formal Italian language throughout his four grades of school in Antrodoco. He put it to use for the first time in Riverside, meeting neighbours from different parts of Italy. He soon learned why the small community had banded together. When my father arrived in Calgary, the city was buzzing with the story of two Italians from British Columbia, Emilio Picariello, an alderman in Blairmore and a rum-runner, and Florence Lassandro, a young woman associated with him. At the Calgary courthouse, they were the centre of a sensational trial that found them guilty of murdering a police officer. They were both sentenced to death, even though it had been twenty-four years since the last woman had been executed in Canada. Now, two Italians were freshly hanged.

People in Riverside were certain that the legal process had been unjust. They contended that key evidence had been covered up and that prejudice doomed the accused from the start. They heard that a group of do-gooder Anglo women, the Famous Five, had worked to spare an Englishwoman the rope. Where were they when Florence needed them?

Wrongly treated or not, the fact that the accused were Italians brought shame upon the Italian communities in western Canada. These communities also feared that news from Italy calling the Italian government "fascist" would tar them, too. At work and at school, hundreds of Italians felt the eyes of others watching them suspiciously. Many people assumed that if two Italians were involved with illegal activities and murder, all Italians were capable of atrocities.

My father learned that life in Calgary had a pecking order of ethnicity, British at the top and Italians near the bottom. In 1921, eighty-two per cent of Calgary's population of 63,305 was British by ethnic origin. The number reflected the effectiveness of federal and provincial laws, as well as the success of CPR programs that paid immigrant families from Britain to farm the prairies. Calgary life was uniformly British, with pockets of Jews, Italians, Chinese, Ukrainians, Germans, and a few others.

Riverside was one of these pockets. People living there didn't think about ethnicity, they thought about survival. In addition to Italians, several Jewish families started out in Riverside, and there was a sprinkling of Irish, German, Polish, Ukrainian, and Russian immigrants both in Riverside and the adjoining community of Bridgeland. They all breathed the same odour from slaughterhouses and garbage

Gisetta and Ricardo Santopinto and family, c. 1935. Standing, from left to right: Ricardo, Frank, Nino, Magi. Seated, from left to right: Jean, Gisetta, Connie.

dumps. Their children went to one of two schools, St. Angela's or Riverside, and most of them collected in the few churches in their neighbourhoods.

Although Gisetta christened her children with Italian names, their teachers at St. Angela's School gave them English names that they carried throughout life. Giannina was called Jean; Concetta became Connie; Nino was changed to Tony; Franco was shortened to Frank. Giuseppe (or Magi, as the family called him) was John in school. This duality was part of their Calgary life: Italian at home and English otherwise.

Genesio knew a few Italians who were starting to move into mainstream Calgary. His friend Jimmy Barbaro joined the Calgary Transit Authority at the bottom of the ladder and over the years climbed the rungs to become the superintendent of Bowness Park in the mid-1930s. It was an important job that carried the responsibility of ensuring that the park, one of the few designed public spaces where British and other immigrants mingled, remained comfortable for all. It was in easy reach, just two tickets on the streetcar, and immigrants could afford to go dancing or canoeing, play midway games, or enjoy a family picnic and then play miniature golf or treat the children to a few rides. Bowness Park fit nicely with the Italian custom of dressing up to go out to meet friends. Young and old Italians, families and singles went there for an outing, and it was large enough that they weren't really noticed by the Anglo visitors.

My father concluded that an anglicized name like Jimmy Barbaro's would make it easier for him to flow in the mainstream. Sam Ross, formerly Salvator Ucci, was a good example of that. An experienced and successful immigrant, Sam clearly saw the merits of a name the locals could pronounce, and so he nudged my father along. In 1929, Genesio tried "Gino," but he didn't like it. "Shorten your name to Gene," advised Gisetta's oldest daughter. "Jean and Gene. We'll sound the same."

My father liked the energetic Gene Tunney, the champion boxer, and Gene Krupa, a talented new drummer on the scene, so he chose "Gene." His family name remained unchanged—it was, after all, the link to his ancestors. Sam said, "Outside Riverside, who can say your name right? Make it easy for them." So Gene allowed his surname to be mispronounced as "See-o-nee" rather than the proper "Ch-o-nee." Years later, after my mother became Mrs. Gene Cioni, following the convention of the day, she said, "Mrs. See-o-nee sounds nicer, softer, than the Italian way." While my father anglicized his name, my mother Americanized it.

It was a warm afternoon at the Millarville races on 10 September 1939.

Ida and Sabatino Cioni with Anna Maria and Gabriele, 14 January 1946.

In the company of Sam and Goldie Ross, the Cionis were celebrating the news of a baby expected in the spring. My father was frustrated with running the small Perfection Store and Ice Cream Parlour, and he hoped that Sam might help him figure out how to get into the real restaurant business. Sam, now a horse owner and trainer, always gave winning advice, particularly at the betting cage. The group strolled across the owners' circle and met star jockey Johnny Longden. Suddenly, over the buzz of the loudspeaker, an agitated voice split the air, "Attention, Attention! Canada's just declared war on Germany."

Martha and Goldie, the Arndt sisters, born of German parents in the United States, and Gene and Sam, immigrants from Italy, suddenly felt very vulnerable. Without doubt they were Canadians, they had lived here as long as anywhere else. Yet their ancestors were Germans and Italians. They saw themselves as Canadians; however, others might not see it the same way.

They discussed how unjust it was that in Canada an immigrant had no citizenship; that is, unless one applied to Britain to become a naturalized subject. "Who wants to be British? We live in Canada!" reasoned my father. "I don't want to become a British subject. To everyone's surprise, including Goldie's, Sam responded with a sheepish grin that in the early 1920s, he had become a naturalized British subject. He explained that he had thought being neutralized would make him equal, but it hadn't.

"I'm not surprised," noted Gene. "This British crap makes me feel like a foreigner and I'm not. I live in Canada and that makes me Canadian."

War brought out the suspicious nature of people, and Gene and Martha wanted their baby to be above suspicion. That is why choosing a name weighed heavily on their minds. They concluded that the name must be simple, strong, and English. Walking back to their apartment after seeing Gary Cooper star in *North West Mounted Police*, they found their answer. In April 1940, they named their newborn son Gary Gene Cioni.

Gary's birth was a bright spot in their lives and in Gene's next letter to Italy he included a photo of his new son. In response, Sabatino sent pictures of his two children, Anna Maria, a toddler and Gabriele, who was already in school in Rome. On 10 June 1940, my parents listened on the radio as Prime Minister King declared that Canada was now at war with Italy. Gene was devastated; it was Fortuna at her cruelest.

It didn't take long for the Canadian government's war procedures to kick in. A letter arrived from Ottawa but my father was too nervous to open the envelope. Mother took it and then read out loud, "Under the authority of the National Resources Mobilization Act and the War Measures Act all persons, sixteen years of age and older, must register with the federal government authorities." Panicking, my father remembered his older half-brothers having to register with the government, signing papers at the city hall, and, shortly after, going into the Italian army. He thought that he might be taken away, leaving his wife and small son to fend for themselves, as had happened when his father died.

"It's okay. We just have to register," Mother reassured him. They decided that she would go first since she looked English, with her piercing blue eyes, light brown hair, and small nose. On 19 August, she wore her wedding outfit as a stylish coat of armour. My father paced and waited. At last, the familiar stride came down the walk.

"What happened?" Gene barked unintentionally, his nerves getting the better of him.

"Here, have a look. It's my National Registration Certificate. It has to be stamped once a year while we're at war. I have to carry it at all times. The form asked for my racial origin. I had to put German." My father covered his ears; he had heard enough. Two days later, it was his turn. He filled in the form, collected his certificate, and left as quickly as he could.

Then another letter from Ottawa. My mother read the contents a few times before she was ready to read the letter to my father. "All persons of German or Italian racial origin, including those who have become naturalized British subjects since September 1, 1929, are now classified as 'enemy aliens.' Enemy aliens must register with the RCMP immediately, thereafter reporting on a monthly basis."

Whether Genesio or Gene, my father was now an enemy alien, and as an Arndt, so was my mother. Their premonition had been right. As far as the Canadian government was concerned, their ancestry trumped their loyalty. For the duration of the war and beyond, they dressed in their best clothes and, with Gary in hand, reported to the police.

When World War II broke out, my father had already lived about the same amount of time in Canada as he had in Italy. He had worked in Calgary, Banff, Lake Louise, Jasper, Trail, Nelson, and Vancouver. Moving around the west, he had come to understand the different regions—the foothills, the Rockies, the interior, and the Pacific coast. He had siblings in Calgary and he had started his own family there. He

Martha and Gene, with Gary in tow, on their way to reporting to police as "enemy aliens," 1944.

belonged in Canada and, in his mind, Calgary was home. So when the government branded him an enemy alien, he felt utterly betrayed by the country he had chosen to be his home.

My parents heard a lot of stories about enemy aliens from fellow immigrants. The Italian, German, and Japanese communities were under suspicion and government surveillance. Shocked Italians witnessed some of their own being rounded up and taken to an internment camp in Kananaskis, in the mountains near Calgary, leaving wives and children to fend for themselves. The Italian community supported these deserted families, without any government help, and they learned that the letters sent to the men from family were censored by the government. For those in the community who had left Italy because of Mussolini, it seemed that there was no escaping him—even in Canada he caused them suffering. They were humiliated that the Canadian government associated them with the dictator.

In fact, the Italian community was fiercely patriotic to Canada. Young men born in Italy volunteered for service but, being enemy aliens, were not accepted. Ironically, months later, some volunteers were conscripted and stationed at bases deemed free of sensitive information.

On the other hand, children born in Calgary of Italian ancestry were allowed to enlist. Many went overseas, including the two Ross boys—Stanley and Harvey—and Gisetta's youngest son, Nino, who lied about his age in order to serve. Nino's passion was photography and he knew that he would make his best contribution as an aerial photographer. When he was declared colour-blind, he inveigled a copy of the test, memorized it, and passed with flying colours. Nino served on many reconnaissance missions over Europe and then took to the ground as the Allies entered the war-ravaged continent. His frontline photos chronicled not only the destruction and desolation, but captured the misery and desperation of survivors. Had they seen these haunting images, Riverside community members would have been crushed.

Meanwhile, the Italian community bought war bonds and worked longer shifts. Several took the additional street car down Fourth Street straight to the Ogden machine shop, where they manufactured arms for the war. After reading a newspaper article on the establishment of a military social club in Calgary, Vincenzo Grassi donated the grand piano that he had bought for his daughter. But being both a patriot and an enemy alien took its toll, creating paranoia in some who thought that severing all connections to Italy was the best way to show unquestioned loyalty to

Gary standing in front of the house in Riverside, 1943.

Canada. Italian was not spoken outside the home. Some families even burned mementoes such as Italian flags, documents, and books, fearing that the Canadian government would confiscate them as evidence of loyalty to Mussolini. Others stopped sending letters to relatives overseas, afraid that the Canadian government was scrutinizing mail.

Gene feared for Sabatino. Still in Rome, he had a job as a streetcar conductor. The two brothers realized that Sabatino could save at least part of his own money to come to Calgary, if that was his family's choice. My father took comfort that neither Sabatino nor his older half-brothers were in the army. He sent letters and packages of food and clothes and prayed that his younger brother had a good chance of surviving the war.

Even as wartime began, a few Italians ventured outside Riverside to establish businesses. Gene's older stepbrother, Reno Corradetti, opened a photography studio downtown, in the east end. *Paesano* Frank Manzara owned the White Dot restaurant next to the Garry Theatre.

After leaving the Perfection Store and Ice Cream Parlour, my father was briefly unemployed. Although there were opportunities outside Calgary for work, he would not leave his young family. Partners in life, my parents decided to be partners in business as well. In 1940, they bought a small Chinese restaurant, the Pacific Lunch, next to the Isis Theatre on 1st Street West and renamed it the Martha Lunch. The long counter had a dozen stools that filled at breakfast, lunch, and after the late-night movie. My father served simple, inexpensive foods such as omelets, soup, sandwiches, meat loaf, pie, and ice cream, which encouraged a rapid turnover of customers that was good for business. It was a sixteen-hour day, punctuated with a kiss and a bit of news as one returned home and the other left for work. They withstood the pace for nearly two years before selling.

For a while my father was out of work, but my mother was welcomed back to Olivier Chocolates, one of her first employers. In August 1942, Gene seized the opportunity through a friend to cook for and manage the dining room at the Shamrock Hotel. He felt Fortuna was on his side; he now had a full kitchen and a good-sized dining room crammed with customers from the Burns Meat Packing plant across the street. He was back to his old form, preparing homemade soups and full-course meals, using his creativity to counter wartime shortages. The flood of Burns employees swelled. A beer from the hotel parlour and Gene's food proved irresistible.

Burns management wanted staff to remain on site, focused on work, not streaming over to the hotel. While having lunch at the Shamrock one day in 1943, the Burns manager found a solution. He hired my father to run the Burns cafeteria. So Gene walked across the street and began cooking for three shifts, for hundreds of workers a day, as the plant operated around the clock to support war needs. My father was proud to be helping Canada's war effort.

Like most families, mine listened to the radio for war updates on the nightly ten o'clock news, eager to hear of a Canadian victory that might bring a quicker end to the war. The year 1943 was particularly tense for my father. He worried about Sabatino as the Allies began to bomb Rome.

When the end of the war finally came, Canadians were worn out, and those of Italian, German, and Japanese descent were also exhausted and demoralized by the long years as enemy aliens. The realization that they were no longer suspect was a great psychological relief to my parents, and the subsequent release of years of tension was even felt by my brother, then five years old. He remembers a marked change in family life—our parents were more relaxed, doing simple things at the spur of the moment. "Let's go for a walk after Sunday Mass and see who we meet," my father would suggest, and off they'd go, hand in hand with Gary.

As part of the end-of-war celebration, my mother's brother, Vernon, an American army veteran from the Saipan campaign, her sister Edna, and Edna's husband, Harry, from the National Guard, came to Calgary to visit their three siblings—my mother, Manuel, and Goldie. When Vernon heard that the three Canadians had to carry documents citing their German racial origin, he shook his head. "What kind of country is this? America calls me a hero and Canada calls you an enemy."

"Let's play cards," said Goldie, "and deal with the future, not the past."

The day before their seventh wedding anniversary, the Cionis read the newspaper headlines announcing that the Liberal government would introduce the Canadian Citizenship Act. Spilling coffee as he jumped up from the table, my father grabbed my mother and waltzed her around the kitchen, newspaper in hand. He read aloud the words of Paul Martin Sr., the minister responsible for the new citizenship act: "Our 'new Canadians' bring to this country much that is rich and good, and in Canada they find a new way of life and new hope for the future. They should all be made to feel that they, like the rest of us, are Canadians, citizens of a great country ..."

"At last!" my father said. Then he sat down and cried.

Prime Minister William Lyon Mackenzie King received citizenship certificate 0001, and in the first wave of applicants, Gene Cioni's Canadian citizenship certificate 16126 took effect 28 November 1947. After twenty-four years of living and working in Canada, he was being recognized as an equal to any other Canadian. Gene was so thankful to the Liberals for realizing the important role of immigrants that he was a card-carrying member of the Liberal Party for the rest of his life.

Gaining citizenship was the high point of 1947; there were also low points. My parents purchased a small diner opposite the Stampede grounds and quickly learned that business was good only during Stampede week and when there were events at the Victoria Pavilion. Although not good for business, the locale offered excitement. Just before Stampede week one year, hundreds of horses were herded down 2nd Avenue, past buildings with windows boarded for safety, into the rodeo pens. My father decided to take Gary and his cousin Marsha to see the animals. No sooner had they reached the infield when a raging bull got loose and started chasing them. Marsha's pink tam flew off and she turned to go back for it, but my father scooped her into one arm without breaking stride. Grabbing

Visiting Sam's race horses, 1946. Left to right: Sam Ross, Goldie Ross, Gene, Martha, Vernon Arndt (U.S. Army). In front: Marsha Ross and Gary.

Gene's Canadian Citizenship Certificate.

Gary's hand, he ran for the fence, diving behind it just in time.

That was my father's last run for awhile. He managed to sell the business and then contracted double pneumonia. A friend gave him the name of a recently arrived physician, Dr. Sid Gelfand, who had spent several years in Canmore caring for miners. The doctor ordered him to rest at home for a few months. "You're worn out, Gene. You've been working too hard."

"Doc, my family needs to eat."

"Then apply for unemployment insurance. If you don't rest, you'll die. What would your family do then?" Gelfand frowned.

Gene had seen first-hand what happened to a family when the father died young. He'd also seen his mother die before she turned fifty, so he knew that he had to listen to the doctor's advice. While Gene rested, Fortuna planned a surprise.

For years, my parents had wanted another baby, but as Martha reached her late thirties they began to think this wouldn't happen. Then she said, "I'm going to make a novena at Our Lady of Perpetual Help Church to pray for a baby."

"But, Marta, you're Lutheran!"

Martha offered the special set of prayers anyway, and waited.

"We're having a novena baby," she said one night at dinner. My father dropped his fork. "God damn it! The novena worked!" he cried as he grabbed her hand and kissed it.

Gene not only wanted another baby, he determined that it had to be a girl. At each monthly visit, my mother proclaimed her positive thoughts, telling the doctor, "We have a wonderful seven-year-old boy and now we're going to have a girl." As the birth date grew closer, the doctor finally retaliated. "What if it's a boy? If it's a boy with red hair like mine, I'll take him."

Concerned at first because there was red hair in her family, my mother maintained her composure. "Oh, it'll be a girl. We're going to name her after my favourite actress, Lana Turner."

In January 1948, I shrieked at the world.

"Pink ribbons!" congratulated the doctor.

Hearing those happy words, my mother succumbed to the anaesthetic. She awoke to find a sobbing husband. "How's our little Lana?" she asked with a note of alarm.

"Lana! Lana! Please, I want to call her Maria. After the Madonna of the Grotto in Antrodoco. This Canadian baby can be proud of an Italian name."

A new routine quickly evolved when the baby came home. While Mother looked after my needs, Father helped Gary get ready for school. After Gary left, Father scanned newspapers, listened to the radio, and talked to people in the Italian community about the post-war situation. He knew that Europe was on the move. Soldiers were returning home, civilians were attempting to re-establish their lives, and refugees were flooding displaced persons' camps. Even though most European countries wanted their citizens to stay and rebuild their countries, Canada reinstituted its pre-war immigration policy to entice people from the United Kingdom, and also committed to taking refugees who had job guarantees. By the late 1940s, only Italy and Holland supported emigration, but the Canadian government wasn't interested in Italians; it preferred Dutch farmers and Americans. It was the intense political pressure from the thousands of Italians living in Canada that finally moved the government to introduce a family sponsorship program.

At the end of the war, the Italian community in Calgary numbered seven hundred. Since it had had no new wave of immigration in the last twenty-two years, it was a small, close-knit community where old customs mixed with modern conveniences in cozy little bungalows that often had a space in the basement for an occasional boarder. Parents spoke Italian to children who answered in English.

Riverside's hilly spine was 4th Street Northeast, along which sat Our Lady of Perpetual Help Church, Picco's Victory Shoe Hospital, Peter Borden's Barbershop, and the Roma Grocery. First Avenue cut across like arms, one arm reaching toward St. Angela's School, the Kozy Lunch, Luke's Drugstore, and several other small stores, and a shorter arm pointing to large rooming houses and the Ukrainian Hall.

This was the Italian community that the first post-war immigrants found as their family sponsors welcomed relatives into a swelling Riverside. These newcomers were different from earlier *paesani*—they were prepared to stay, many of them coming with their families. Some had fought in the war as far away as Russia, some were sons of farmers who had lost everything, others were gifted trade and craft workers. As well, Italians from Toronto and Montreal were also heading for Calgary, hearing that the new oil discoveries meant jobs and business opportunities. Then, too, there was the usual flow of Italians in and out of British Columbia.

The rejuvenated Italian community vibrated with energy. Children born in Calgary of earlier Italian immigrants were now young adults, working in retail and business offices and studying in trades and professions. Many were single with incomes and the desire to enjoy themselves.

Calgarians were returning to a normal life. Even though money was tight, people were becoming adventurous and ready to release pent-up emotion. Veterans had returned from the European battle front with broader perspectives. Some had fought in the Italian campaign on the barren land that in another time would have seduced them. Returnees were eager to rejoin or start families, better their education, and work toward a rewarding future. The Calgary that they returned to was different, transformed by the economic surge that would continue through the Fabulous Fifties and sweep the citizens of Calgary along with it.

Calgary was opening up to the world. While Edmonton had become the gateway to the north, Calgary was the natural southern connection between Montreal or Toronto, and Vancouver. Rail links, commerce, and travel expanded southward to Seattle, San Francisco, and Los Angeles, and Italian foods and restaurants in these cities became a source of inspiration and ideas for my father.

The major American oil and gas companies sent executives from California, Oklahoma, Kansas, Colorado, Illinois, New York, and Texas to establish corporate offices in Calgary. Coming from the affluent United States, they demanded the lifestyle they had enjoyed in Houston, Denver, Chicago, New York, Los Angeles, and Tulsa: a rhythm of working hard during the week and dressing up for a night on the town with friends on the weekend.

In November 1948, 250 Stampeder football fans boarded a special thirteen-car train to Toronto to cheer their team to Grey Cup victory. With horses, chuckwagons, and a western music trio featuring Bill Galiardi on accordion, revellers in Stetsons sashayed, some on horseback, into Union Station and the Royal York Hotel. Other fans set up chuckwagons in the financial district, flipping pancakes and serving barbecued ribs to bewildered Toronto executives. Hundreds more Stampeder fans arrived by chartered plane. They put the east on notice: Calgary was an energetic city where the quality of life kept pace with the steaming economy. The Stampeders and their fans returned victorious, and Calgarians had a newfound identity. They were going places.

Gene could see that his new Italian restaurant could be one of those places. Calgary seemed ready for a restaurant specializing in Italian food. He was certainly ready! He had come of age as a cook and manager in Calgary; he understood the mood of the city and seized the opportunity. Gene envisioned American executives, business people, soldiers, the Stampeders and their fans, the established Italian community, and newcomers all dining on his Calgary cooking—Italian style. He consulted relatives and trusted friends and was overwhelmed by their enthusiasm. A *paesano*, Vittorio Cioni, loaned Gene a few thousand dollars, and another *paesano*, Louis Carloni, said that he could rent the basement of an apartment house he owned in Riverside.

Although my father was estranged from his stepfather, Annibale Corradetti, he remained in close contact with the Corradetti offspring. His oldest half-brother, Nick, was a contractor. "Can you make a restaurant in the basement?" Gene asked Nick.

"It'll be a tiny kitchen," replied Nick. "You might fit eight tables."

"How fast can you do it? And can I pay you half now and half after I'm opened for a few months?"

"Jesus, Gene!" exclaimed Nick. "You're lucky I'm your brother."

My father knew that choosing the right name for his restaurant was important. It had to entice customers with something familiar, yet new. The only familiar Italian food in Calgary was canned spaghetti, which Heinz advertised as a "quick-fix meal for housewives." The heat-and-serve contents were unrecognizable to Italians, just as Gene's spaghetti would be foreign to most Calgarians.

Gene's Spaghetti Parlor, Calgary's first Italian restaurant, was officially opened in March 1949, at 111A–4 Street Northeast. Situated in the midst of the Italian community that had been my father's home since 1923, Gene's restaurant was open to all Calgarians no matter what their name.

SPAGHETTI WESTERN

The Good, the Bad and the Ugly

—A Sergio Leone movie

MY MOTHER phoned in the wording for the first advertisement in the *Calgary Herald*, and on 2 March, my father flipped to the entertainment page. "Shit," he snarled as he read: "Jeanes' Spaghetti Parlor.""What the hell! People are going to think a woman owns my restaurant." My mother phoned the newspaper to set matters straight. It re-ran the ad without charge. Mother could laugh about the incident, but Father always cursed when he was reminded of it.

Thereafter, the proper ad ran regularly in the Wednesday and weekend editions, inviting people to come for a late dinner "after the show." Late-night Italian dining and dancing was a new alternative to expensive, formal dinners at the Palliser Hotel or quick, casual meals at a Chinese restaurant. At 8 PM, the evening was just getting started at Gene's, but at other restaurants, such as the Tea Kettle Inn and the Carolina, the doors were being locked.

Word of Gene's flew through Riverside and across the river into the business community. Even on the coldest wintry nights, forty guests filled the spaghetti parlour, and on weekend nights, more than a hundred crowded in. A blackboard outside the kitchen listed Gene's three main dishes: spaghetti and meatballs, meat ravioli, and chicken cacciatore. For $1.50, customers enjoyed not only the main course, but soup, salad, and dessert. When he wasn't cooking, my father was in the dining room welcoming and chatting with his customers. His gregarious personality, wit, and charming accent were as much of a draw as his delicious food.

On 23 June 1949, a frenzy swept through the neighbourhood. The former World Heavyweight Boxing Champion and Italian superstar wrestler Primo Carnera was in town. Carnera had started his boxing career in Europe before heading to America, where he earned nearly a million dollars from 1928 to 1934, only to be bilked by crooked managers. He returned to Italy penniless in 1937 and joined a resistance movement. He was later captured by Mussolini's state police and put in a labour camp. Returning to America after the war, he found fame as a wrestler. Now, Primo Carnera had come to Calgary as the main draw on the wrestling card, and he was heading to Gene's.

Carnera entered the restaurant, size thirteen shoes first, then the six foot seven frame, folding to duck through the door. My father stretched his arm up to shake the famous hand and seated him near the kitchen. "My menu is small but it's good Abruzzese food," gushed my father.

"I like everything"—Carnera smiled—"especially Abruzzese-style, even though I come from Udine."

"*Perfetto!*" responded my father. "Leave it to me."

The neighbourhood was buzzing, and now people swarmed the small restaurant hoping to see the celebrity. My father pushed through the crowd to telephone my mother with the news. These days she stayed home looking after Gary and me, doing the restaurant bookkeeping, and washing the checkered linen tablecloths when we went to bed. Then Gene phoned Nino, the veteran army photographer. "Come quick! Primo Carnera's here," he shouted. Nino came running, camera in hand.

"Can I get a photo of you in the kitchen with my uncle?" Nino asked the celebrity. Carnera obliged. His head skimmed the ceiling as he posed with the five foot six cook, who barely reached his shoulder. Then he good-naturedly posed with other *paesani* and signed autographs until he smelled the food. My father carried the largest platter in the restaurant to his guest. Gene had prepared all three specialties, and Carnera devoured every one. "*Grazie*, Gene. I'll see you next time I'm in town."

After that magnificent night, more sports personalities came— wrestlers, football players, hockey players, and jockeys. One evening, some champion Stampeder football players arrived. Paul Rowe, the star fullback, took my father aside. "Listen, Gene, I have someone outside. He's with us. He's one of the boys. Will you let him in?"

Bewildered, my father put a hand on Paul's shoulder. "Any law-abiding person is welcome in my place."

In came Woody Strode, the all-star who had scored the winning touchdown in the 1948 Grey Cup game. Woody was tall and muscular—and black. My father welcomed him. When the 1949 football season started, Woody brought in his friend and new Stampeder Sugarfoot Anderson. The two came so often that Gene offered, "My restaurant is your home. I'll make dishes that aren't on the menu so you don't get bored." Having been stereotyped and declared an enemy alien, my father had resolved to rise above prejudice in his own dealings. There was no colour barrier in Gene's restaurant.

Neither was there religious prejudice. Gene's inviting welcome and good food attracted many, and the Jewish community especially loved my father. Billy Belzberg, a young man about town, showed up one night with half a dozen of his pals. They stashed their brown paper bags with liquor under the tabletop, where the carpenter had made a small ledge just the right size for a bottle of whisky or wine.

By closing time, the Belzberg party had eaten, and their liquor bottles were emptied. My father had taken off his apron and sat with them in the dining room, joking and telling outlandish stories. Then Billy eyed the red-checkered tablecloth. "Gene, I've always wanted to try the trick, you know, you pull the tablecloth off the table, leaving the dishes. Can I try?"

Gene welcomes Italian boxing legend Primo Carnera to his first restaurant, 23 June 1949.

No sooner had my father shrugged his shoulder than dishes, glasses, jangling silverware, and bits of food flew through the air, crashing against the wall and shattering on the floor. There was stunned silence and then my father burst into laughter. "You need more practice," he said, getting the broom. "Maybe at another restaurant!"

Each night my father emptied the till and filled a brown paper bag, securing it with an elastic band. He took it home to the small bungalow at the top of the 4th Street hill and left it on the kitchen table. In the morning, after Gary had left for school, my mother tallied the money and paid the bills. In less than six months, Gene and Martha could see that their dream was taking hold—the restaurant was making a profit. If the crowds continued, they would consider a bigger venue.

On a sunny autumn morning, my father stopped to visit Gisetta. Like everyone else in Riverside, they talked about the "new" Italians. "More from Antrodoco," said Gene. "Two more Brandelli brothers coming soon."

"The Manzaras are sponsoring the Zaghetto family," added Gisetta. "I heard there's a list of people now who'll take boarders. Everyone wants to help. What about Sabatino? Does he want to come?"

Gene had never had enough extra money to bring his younger brother to Calgary. Sabatino's life was in Italy; the brothers were resigned to the idea that the Cioni family would have an ocean between them.

"He's doing all right in Rome."

"What'll you do to help out?" Gisetta asked.

"I have no money but I have lots of food. I'll feed them."

"I hear there's also a list for interpreters who'll translate for the newcomers at job interviews," said Gisetta. "I thought about it, but not after hearing Mary Cioni's stories. She told me about filling out job applications for newcomers. There's a lot of prejudice in town. Some employers ripped up the applications when they saw the Italian names. She even heard them shout, 'Get out, bum!'"

The three Brandelli brothers—Ivo, Adelmo, and Mario—were fortunate to have the help of many Antrodocani in the community to settle in, including my father. Ivo, who was in his mid-twenties and had fought in Russia, had come first in 1948. He worked with Nick Corradetti building Gene's Spaghetti Parlor. Adelmo and Mario, who had been in the Italian navy, arrived in early 1949. All three lived in the apartment above the restaurant.

My father took the Brandelli brothers under his wing. When the pasta e fagioli soup, their favourite, was ready, he tapped the ceiling with the broom handle. They charged down to the restaurant for a free meal with Gene before the customers came. Through the Brandellis, my father reconnected to his hometown. "Tell me, is so-and-so still alive? Are couples still sneaking to *il Buco di Baciafemmina* to kiss?"

After closing the restaurant at three in the morning, my father sometimes stopped by to visit the brothers, always with a plate in his hands. "Close your eyes and taste this," he would instruct. "What does it remind you of?"

"Antrodoco!" they laughed.

"Here's a deal. I'll feed you, and when I need help, you'll work a little in the restaurant."

So on weekends and sometimes on Wednesdays, Adelmo answered Gene's call. He put on his suit pants, rolled up his white shirt sleeves, and brushed back his wavy hair. Gene handed him an apron. "Don't worry. You don't need to speak English. Just serve the food with a smile and clear away the dirty dishes."

Adelmo was a quick study. Soon he could swivel between the tables with a full tray and weave around dancers to reach the kitchen. He listened closely to the way Gene talked and laughed with the customers, whether Italian or not. Adelmo watched as patrons ate Italian food with gusto, poured drinks from the bottles under the table, and danced till the early hours. They even stole little kisses while dancing. They were acting like Italians.

Nightly, Louis Carloni witnessed the numbers of people entering the basement of his building. A wily man, he could see that Gene's Spaghetti Parlor was outgrowing the location. Louis made my father a proposal. He and his nephew, Leo Fabbi, would renovate the building next door to make a large ground-floor restaurant that he would lease to Gene. Louis and his nephew would take care of the building and operate the banquet rooms on the first and second floor. My father trusted Louis Carloni. No written agreement was necessary for these traditional *paesani*, and so their business deal was sealed with a handshake. In September 1949, Louis obtained a city permit to convert the building.

My father knew precisely what to call his second restaurant— Gene's Spaghetti Dine and Dance. The elegant expression "dine and dance" had enthralled my father since he first saw it in Vancouver in the

1930s. In Calgary there was Peneley's, a dance hall, and the Palliser Hotel, which held supper dances a couple of times a week. My father initiated dining and dancing at Gene's until the wee hours of the morning, five nights a week; he attracted customers to an event, not just a fine meal.

After only nine months, Gene closed down the first restaurant in mid-December, leaving just two weeks to move into the new location. Again, he hired Nick Corradetti to construct the second restaurant, and this time he was able to pay his brother on time.

The New Year's Eve celebrations on 31 December 1949, marked the opening of Gene's Spaghetti Dine and Dance. Hours before revellers arrived, friends were painting the handrail as Nick hung the lights. Crowds flowed in. They partied—food, drinks, dancing—and at midnight they cheered the end of a decade of war. Calgary and Gene were racing into the Fabulous Fifties.

As my father had promised, he helped new Italian immigrants by feeding them. During the week, unemployed single men met at the church hall to play cards and bocce and eat sandwiches made by the ladies' group. Some availed themselves of the opportunity to learn English. Because the church schedule was filled with weddings and baptisms on Saturdays and Sundays, my father

Bill Galiardi entertains at Mr. and Mrs. Louie Carloni's 25th wedding anniversary party held at Gene's Spaghetti Parlor, December 1948.

invited them to Gene's Dine and Dance on weekend afternoons. While he started dinner preparations, they played cards. Soon the local community came as well, accompanying the family members they had sponsored, and they all ate and danced.

The reputation of the new Gene's snowballed, and Louis was the beneficiary as Gene's popularity helped fill his banquet rooms. At times the building was a schizophrenic scene: Gene serving Italian food to the social set in his restaurant, while above, in Louis's L.C. Ballroom, singles came to drink and party at a square dance or Latin night with Ray Valdez and his Calgary Stampeders Orchestra—gents, 75¢, ladies, 50¢. Sometimes weddings or corporate parties were held in the banquet rooms, and on those occasions Gene catered the dinner.

By December 1950, Louis had turned the first floor of banquet rooms into the Clover Club, offering a New Year's Eve floor show, turkey supper, and orchestra for twelve dollars per couple. Gene's also offered New Year's celebrations, featuring turkey dinner and dancing for eight dollars per couple. They were now competing businesses.

Without a written agreement, Gene and Louis had different ideas regarding their deal, as well as conflicting priorities and personalities. Gene was the best chef in Calgary.

Gene's Dine and Dance
request the honour of your presence
at
the Banquet on the occasion of their
Official Opening
Tuesday, February 28th, 1950
at 6:30 P. M.
109 Fourth Street North East, Calgary

Gene hosts family and friends from Antrodoco in a party room above Gene's Spaghetti Dine and Dance, c. summer 1950.

He had built his reputation by insisting on using fine products, such as Unico brand, which cost him more because he had to import Unico products from Toronto. Louis, on the other hand, was focused on one thing: making a profit at every turn. Father was annoyed that Louis was increasingly on the premises of Gene's, notwithstanding that Gene was the lessee.

Gene's Dine and Dance was bursting with customers, but on some nights, Mother found that the money in the till was less than the billings. She alerted my father. "Gene, there's something wrong. Watch who's going into the till. Who's got keys to our restaurant?" There were more unexplained losses throughout the business; stock and food supplies were even disappearing overnight.

My father's stress mounted as he felt his formerly tight control over his restaurant business slipping. He became edgy and unhappy. One day he asked Louis, "You're around all the time. What's going on?" Louis gave no answers. Becoming increasingly frustrated that these problems were diverting his concentration from his cooking, one day Gene marched upstairs to get answers from Louis.

Once he started, he couldn't stop. The voices got louder, tempers flared, and all the differences and pent-up emotions between the two men erupted. At the breaking point, my father knew he had to leave, to walk away from the building. He told Louis that their agreement was over. Louis challenged Gene, saying that if he left, he would go with nothing.

Less than two years before, Gene had opened his Dine and Dance and it had quickly grown into a fifties' hot spot that was crammed every night, but that day in August 1951, he walked out and never returned.

The blood drained from his face as he climbed the long hill home. With anger welling inside him, he relived the blowout, telling Martha that Louis had scoffed, "Go! But your name stays here. This is the only Gene's!"

Martha knew that Gene's name was their family's future and that they needed the best lawyer in town to fight Louis. "A bad agreement is better than a good lawsuit," says the Italian proverb. Italians had a deep distrust of lawyers and a firm conviction to keep business private, but this was Canada, and Martha was angry and scared.

"I think I know a good lawyer," she said. "When I worked at Puss'n Boots, the young lawyers from the Lougheed Building used to come in for lunch. I knew one of the lawyers, Billy Epstein, whose family lived by the Rosses. He introduced me to Harold Riley. I've read about Riley in the newspaper. I'll call Billy's mother and see how Billy's doing in his new job at the United Nations and then ask her about Riley."

Harold Riley was to the point. "What do you want? Money? The restaurant? Louis has no business in your restaurant other than arranged appointments as the landlord. We can keep him out of your business."

"I only want my name. I want my name for my next restaurant."

1
0
9

4th

S

T

|Six|

IN 1949, when Gene opened his first Italian restaurant, he wanted his customers to enjoy the authentic taste of his cooking, so he chose to offer just a few well-prepared dishes. As he introduced new tastes to his customers, tantalizing their palates, he kept note of their preferences so that in the future he could dip into his Abruzzese culture for more offerings.

Gene's small menu reflected the limitations of his spaghetti parlour. The restaurant was so small that he had limited space in which to cook and store ingredients. He took advantage of this, though, making a wide doorway between the kitchen and dining room, allowing guests to see him cook their orders.

Gene started his dinners with homemade soup, knowing that the intensely distilled flavour would activate customers' taste buds. Each day he turned cold water, bones, vegetables, and herbs into mouth-watering stracciatella, minestrone, or turkey soup with rice. On Fridays, he made pasta e fagioli, a hearty macaroni and cannellini bean soup, and for weekends, chicken brodo with tiny pasta pieces.

Music inspired my father as he cooked. He loved opera and jazz and made sure that the Wurlitzer jukebox service stocked his favourites, such as Louis Armstrong. He sang and danced as he waited for his soup to come to a boil. As he removed the lid, the escaping steam pushed the aroma throughout the restaurant and through the ceiling into the apartments above.

My father prepared the spaghetti sauce of his childhood, but in

EATING CULTURE

WHAT IS THE GLORY OF
DANTE COMPARED TO
SPAGHETTI?

—G. Prezzolini, *Maccheroni & C*

Calgary he was thrilled to improve the richness with a quality of beef not found in Italy. Italians held the tomato sauce of Abruzzo in high regard because of the lush taste of the local tomatoes, sweetened by hours of sun. Although Canadian tomatoes were much cheaper, my father insisted on using Abruzzese Italian plum tomatoes canned by Unico and shipped from Toronto. He had no written recipe for the sauce, and only my mother knew the ingredients, the proportions, and the cooking techniques that rendered the unique taste that became the signature of Gene's success.

Six days a week, my father swung his twenty-four-quart stainless steel pot on to a burner and, to the strains of Verdi, began to prepare his sauce. He always selected an Italian composer to listen to while he made the sauce. As the olive oil heated, he flattened cloves of garlic, then added them to the pot. When they were golden, he removed them and added lightly salted chunks of beef or veal as well as some pork ribs, stirring the meat until it was bronze. He chopped large measures of onions, celery, and green peppers, sliding them alongside the meat to wilt. Then he crushed dried chili peppers, several bay leaves, oregano, basil, and rosemary by rubbing them between the palms of his hands to release flavour as they dropped into the pot. He added a bit of salt to the savoury herbs and nippy spices and much more ground black pepper, a commodity that Romans prized as much as gold.

Gene crushed the Italian plum tomatoes through his fingers, careful to hold back the seeds. The sauce grew crimson as he stirred in the tomato paste, and when the mixture became dark and lush, he poured in four large cans of tomato juice and when the liquid came back to a boil he lowered the gas, leaving the tastes to condense to subtle perfection. Just fifteen minutes before the sauce was ready, Gene added sliced mushrooms.

My father selected Coleman Hawkins's "Body and Soul" on the Wurlitzer and moved on to make the meatballs. He mixed a smaller portion of the fattier ground pork with several pounds of minced veal or minced beef, to provide a moist, complex taste. Into the large stainless steel mixing bowl, he added finely diced celery, green peppers, and onions to broaden the flavour, and then fistfuls of minced parsley, dried herbs, and generous amounts of salt and pepper. He threw in handfuls of bread crumbs and some beaten eggs to bind the mixture, and then—his secret touch—a bit of tomato juice for additional moisture and tang.

Gene's Spaghetti Sauce

(Serves 100)

1 head garlic, cloves peeled and smashed
flat with the flat edge of a chopping knife

5 lb. each beef and veal (use cheaper cuts)

4 lb. pork spareribs (the more meat, the
richer the sauce)

6 onions, finely chopped

12 sticks celery, finely chopped

2 carrots, finely chopped

6 fistfuls each dried basil, oregano, and
rosemary

8 large bay leaves

2 100 fl. oz. cans Unico plum tomatoes

28 fl. oz. can Unico tomato paste

4 100 fl. oz. cans tomato juice

2 lb. mushrooms, sliced

salt and black pepper

A 46-quart pot is an ideal size in which to make sauce for one hundred people. Cover the bottom of the pot with olive oil and heat. Add garlic, removing when golden brown.

Add meat and a generous amount of black pepper. Brown the meat, scraping up any bits that stick to the pot. Remove meat and set aside. Add onions and sauté for 15 minutes. Add other vegetables and sauté until wilted. Rub herbs between palms and drop into the pot with the bay leaves. Stir until herbs are well cooked with vegetables.

Squeeze the seeds out of the canned tomatoes, then crush the tomatoes before dropping them into the pot. Stir until mixture bubbles, about 15 minutes.

Add tomato paste. When dark crimson and bubbling, add tomato juice and bring to a boil. Return browned meat to sauce. Simmer for 4½ hours, uncovered. Remove meat and add mushrooms. Return to simmer for 15 minutes, uncovered.

When sauce has cooked, add salt and pepper to taste. Turn heat off and cover until ready to use.

Sliding his wedding ring into his apron pocket, Gene launched his short, thick fingers into the mass. Working to the beat of the Hawkins saxophone, he swept his arms around the bowl, drawing the ingredients to the middle and back through his fingers until he could feel they were mixed just right. He rolled small handfuls of meat between his palms and dropped the smooth orbs onto waxed paper.

Next came the tricky part. My father had to shift the pot of cooling soup to the sink draining board to make room for his cast-iron frying pans. He browned dozens of plump meatballs, drained the fat, and slipped them into the spaghetti sauce. He always stood for a few minutes to watch as they surrendered their juices to the sauce.

Gene had learned the art of making meatballs from the Pini family in Vancouver. More recently, Tony Pini and his wife, Stella, had opened the Barn Restaurant, near Granville Street, in 1947 and become famous for their meatballs. Meatballs were not part of the Antrodoco tradition. As far as Gene knew, they were an American inspiration, but the customers found them different, delicious, and fun to eat. My father liked to make them, too, not only because they were easy to prepare, but because he had only a three-burner stove and the meatballs shared the same pot as the sauce.

Just before six o'clock, a pot of cold water was put on the third burner to heat. When an order for spaghetti or ravioli came into the kitchen, my father added a large pinch of salt to the boiling water and gradually stirred in one fistful of spaghetti per order. After seven minutes, he tasted a strand to ensure that it was tender but firm, *al dente*, then he quickly strained the rest, putting them back in the original pot with a little sauce. My father insisted on warmed plates to serve his spaghetti, along with two meatballs placed together on the right side, and, finally, just a small dollop of extra sauce on top. Gene didn't believe in excess and never served spaghetti drowning in sauce; he scooped just enough sauce to sweeten the pasta. Cheese was grated every day to keep the fresh tangy flavour and served in a little bowl so customers could help themselves.

Intuitively, this cook understood that contrasting tastes inspired the taste buds. To complement the sweetness of the tomato sauce, he wanted cheese that was salty yet rich in flavour, so he mixed Romano cheese, a hard sheep's milk variety, with the more mellow aged Parmesan. Gene cut large chunks daily and, just as in an Italian household, he gave his son the honour of grating it whenever he was at the restaurant. The instructions were simple: "Grate right down to the rind but watch your fingers." Cheese is expensive. We can't afford to waste any. By the age of nine, Gary was a grating aficionado whose reward was eating the succulent thin, salty pieces of rind.

Gene's third specialty was chicken cacciatore. Contrary to the practice in Antrodoco, my father left the tomatoes out of this dish. Since both his spaghetti and ravioli had tomato sauce, he decided that the cacciatore would have a very different taste. He created a spicy chicken sautéed in olive oil with oregano, onions, peppers, and mushrooms.

After a few months, he introduced a further innovation. By leaving the vegetables out, he created fried chicken Gene's style that was simplicity itself. Dusting a half chicken in flour, he pan-fried it in olive oil with a hint of garlic, oregano, salt, and pepper, resulting in Italian-spiced, crispy-skinned chicken without batter or deep-frying.

The larger kitchen that Nick Corradetti had built at Gene's Spaghetti Dine and Dance expanded my father's culinary universe. By now, he had a pretty good knowledge of his customers' tastes. In response, he created a menu of both traditional Abruzzi food and Calgarian dishes, prepared in Gene's Italian way. My

Gene's Chicken Cacciatore

(Serves 1)

1 whole chicken leg (thigh and drumstick)

flour

olive oil

dried oregano

1 tsp. butter

¼ tsp. minced garlic

¼ small onion, sliced

¼ small green pepper, sliced

1/3 c. sliced mushrooms

½ tsp. chopped anchovies

salt and pepper

Rinse the chicken and pat dry. Lightly dust it in flour, shake off excess, sprinkle one side with oregano and sauté in medium-hot olive oil, turning as the skin becomes crispy and brown. Cook for about 8 minutes per side. Remove the chicken to a warm dish.

Add butter to the same pan and cook garlic, onion, green pepper, and mushrooms for 3 minutes. Return the chicken to the pan, add anchovies, stir, and cook for another 2 minutes. Add salt and pepper to taste and serve.

Gene toasts that the newlyweds, Jean and Jack Amantea, have a life of happiness, 19 August 1950.

father was eager to serve steak, Calgary's favourite food. The quality and availability of Alberta beef was a luxury unknown in Abruzzo. To do justice to this fine meat, my father ordered a specially made grill. However, problems with venting caused smoke to seep into the dining room. When my father heard how much it would cost for a new ventilation system, he declared that the smoke enhanced the atmosphere, and the grill stayed.

My father used only the highest grade of meat, Red Brand, and selected the T-bone cut, part tender fillet, part marbled, juicy loin. He wanted to put his own brand on the steaks—to grill them in Gene's style—so he rubbed each steak with garlic and olive oil just before placing them on the grill. When they were done, he sprinkled salt and pepper on the steaks and let them sit for a couple of minutes so that the meat absorbed the juices. But still my father wasn't satisfied. He felt that the richness of the meat needed to be balanced and remembered the earthy flavour of the many varieties of mushrooms that grew wild in the woods surrounding Antrodoco. This being Calgary, he sautéed cultivated mushrooms in olive oil with a touch of garlic and created the perfect accompaniment to the steak.

My father was dismayed to find that some of his customers had little appreciation of how a good steak should taste. "I prefer my steak blue," ordered one woman.

Gene knew that the steak wouldn't even be hot. "Please, try it medium-rare." Returning with a platter, he handed the steak knife to the petite carnivore and waited until he saw the surprised flash in her eyes as the hot juices filled her mouth.

"What do you think?" he asked.

"Delicious," she acquiesced.

"Cook my steak well. I don't want to see any red," ordered another customer.

"You need to have a little pink for taste. Try it medium." Father purposely chose not to say medium-rare. "It's on the house if you don't like it." Delivering the platter, the cook waited as the slightly pink piece of meat was cautiously chewed—then, the appreciative smile.

In a city where steak was the preferred meat, my father introduced his personal style to local dishes. Gene's treatment of both the familiar and the foreign was an revolution in Calgary dining that became known as "Gene's style."

My father added breaded veal cutlet Milanese to his menu. He pounded the veal paper thin and dipped it in egg, then bread crumbs, before sautéing it. He finished with a squirt of lemon. The delicate taste of the meat could not have been more different from steak. Veal Milanese was such a big hit, particularly with female customers, that my father expanded his menu. He added seasonal dishes such as spring lamb chops grilled with lemon and herbs, accompanied by the signature pastas. Gene appreciated that teaming spaghetti and ravioli with the main course meats made it imperative that the amount of spaghetti sauce didn't overwhelm the rest of the meal.

When Italians ate at Gene's Dine and Dance, they usually ordered in stages: antipasto, a starter; primo, usually pasta; secondo, the main course; and dolci, dessert. My father knew that the Italian approach was too unfamiliar, so he translated the Italian culinary habits into an offering he called "the deluxe dinner."

The deluxe dinner included an appetizer of homemade chicken soup with small egg noodles. To follow, Gene offered his latest creation, the anchovy salad. He dressed crunchy iceberg lettuce (the only variety then available), cucumber, green spring onion, and tomatoes with an olive oil and lemon vinaigrette. For Calgarians used to mayonnaise-based dressings, the light, fruity vinaigrette, an Antrodoco staple, tantalized the taste buds. Guests sopped up the excess dressing with a roll. My father crowned the salad with two giant black olives along with the featured ingredient, an anchovy fillet. He knew that its spiny saltiness and pungent taste would make a simple salad memorable.

Because salad was the main vegetable, my father bought the best available lettuce, tomatoes, and cucumber all year round. In the event that the produce was below his standards, he could always add a few more black olives and an extra anchovy. My father gave considerable thought to when to serve the salad. Calgarians usually ate salad with the main course, while Italians preferred it after. Gene determined that a modest-sized salad would follow the soup. Just as in Roman times, it would awaken the appetite for the main course.

Antrodoco was a town rich in desserts, but my father didn't have the patience to measure the exact amounts required in baking. So he bought imported Italian Gorgonzola cheese, shipped from Toronto, and ice cream with strawberry topping. He hired an Italian woman to make a custard zabaglione and a walnut torta. Traditionally, he would have used the plentiful almonds of Abruzzo in the torta, but in Calgary he replaced them with the less expensive, fresher California walnuts. Gene thought that customers might find espresso too strong, so to settle the meal he served a medium-roast coffee from Tuxedo Coffee and Spice Mills near Riverside, the only roasting facility in Calgary.

My father didn't have the luxury of a wide selection of imported foods that are readily available today. When I read his menu and deconstruct his dishes, I can appreciate how he developed his offerings to accommodate not only local taste buds, but also the availability of products. My father was devoted to finding the best quality ingredients, but he was also realistic in substituting local and available products. There was nothing haphazard about his cooking or his menu. Gene gave much thought to how to balance ingredients in making his dishes and how those dishes complemented each other in the various courses. While his passion was to serve tantalizing Italian cuisine, he was a businessman whose self-directed guideline was ten percent profit above the cost of ingredients and the operation of the restaurant. Gene's formula and philosophy, rooted in his talent and experience, revolutionized Calgary's culinary culture. With the introduction of Gene's cooking, there was no turning back.

La Villa opposite the Shaganappi Golf Course at 33rd Street SW, summer 1952.

|Seven|

❧ LA VILLA ❧

DIFFERENT PLACES ON THE
FACE OF THE EARTH HAVE
DIFFERENT VITAL EFFLUENCE,
DIFFERENT VIBRATION,
DIFFERENT CHEMICAL
EXHALATION, DIFFERENT
POLARITY WITH DIFFERENT
STARS: CALL IT WHAT YOU
LIKE. BUT THE SPIRIT OF
PLACE IS A GREAT REALITY.

—D. H. Lawrence,
Studies in Classic American Literature

A LARGE BUILDING, acreage, and a location as far away from the Italian community as possible—these were the criteria that my parents gave to the real estate agent. Driving from the southwest city limits back into downtown Calgary on a bleak afternoon in late November 1951, the agent suddenly stopped, just past a beat-up for sale sign. Rolling down the window, she craned her neck to get a better view of the dilapidated two-storey house.

"Look," said my father, "there's a chicken coop and a barn."

The clients started whispering. They got out, found an opening in the overgrown hedge, and climbed through for a better look. Gone for a good fifteen minutes, they returned, walking past the car into the middle of the potholed road. There, making a slow 360° turn, all they saw was the Shaganappi Municipal Golf Course immediately opposite. Settling back into the car, my father tapped the agent's shoulder. "We're interested."

As the car picked up speed, Gene took his wife's gloved hand. For the majority of his life, he had been on a whirlwind journey: leaving Antrodoco to begin a life in Calgary, finding and losing his mother, training as a barber, but achieving success as a cook. Discovering this property gave him the comforting feeling that he need travel no farther. He sensed an opportunity, albeit a risky one, to settle down with his family and his business, all under one roof.

That evening, in the kitchen of their small bungalow, my parents were deep into one of those rare conversations that changes the course of one's life. My mother sat calmly considering, but my father jumped up, running his hand from the bald top of his head down to the soft black waves behind his ear. "We need music." Whether it was opera or popular songs by Mario Lanza, Jan Peerce, or Nat King Cole, music soothed my father's soul. At the phonograph, he lowered the needle. A brief hiss, the strings began, and my father was able to relax.

They sat on the cut-velvet sofa, facing each other. "When I was eight years old," began my father, taking my mother's hand, "I borrowed a friend's bicycle. For the first time I felt unconfined by the streets of my town. I remember racing along the Via Salaria—the old Roman salt road. My heart was pounding. Then the long ascent into the Apennine hills. There, I discovered the Villa Mentuccia and, I swear to God, I still remember every detail. I'd never seen anything so big. So much open space. When I close my eyes, I can still see the top of the big house against the mountains. The olive and chestnut groves flowing up the hill. At the back of the villa, there was a courtyard, a barn, and a chicken run. I was surprised to see it was a working farm.

"Where I come from, only a very few families have the means to own a villa. We were just fragments of a family. My father died young; I still don't know the details. When my mother left Sabatino and me with our grandmother and uncle, I had no idea how far away she was going. Her words still blow in my ear, 'I'll send for you soon.' I lived for nearly seven years on that promise, my life on hold. I dreamed of my brother and me joining our mother. In Canada, we'd be a happy family again. Every spring and fall, I trudged up the mountains to the shrine of the Madonna of the Grotto. I looked for knee prints, figuring others had found a good spot to pray. As the years passed, I began to lose heart. 'Mary, Mother of God, make my dreams real! Help me get rich so that one day I can buy a villa and have a home for my family to live.'"

My father took a few deep breaths. "Maybe the property we saw today is the villa I prayed for."

Martha held her husband. "Let's have a good look at that property," she said, kissing his cheek. "Then we'll decide."

A few days later, after Sunday Mass, my father backed the '48 Dodge sedan out of the garage. Gary slid in beside him, then mother, with me on her lap. We picked up Manuel, my mother's brother, his wife, Annie, and their teenage daughter, Marina, and then headed across town.

Driving past the new million-dollar Crippled Children's Hospital, Aunt Annie asked, "How many people do you know who got polio?"

Mother shuddered. "Too many." Every time my mother read about a polio outbreak at schools and other public places, she gave us her remedy. She put crushed garlic into our tomato juice or wrapped it in a piece of bread to trick us.

We stopped at Cuddie's Corner on 29th Street, at the end of the paved road. It seemed the last outpost of civilization, the end of the Killarney bus line. To reach the villa from here, we travelled more than a mile on the gravel road. We didn't know that in springtime cars on this road would be up to their hubcaps in mud; in summer, relentless dust would coat the inside of the windshields; and in winter, the snow would have to be shovelled off the road by hand.

At 33rd Street, a large sign announced "The Calgary Gun Club, Members Only." Then the Shaganappi Municipal Golf Course came into view and, finally, the villa property.

My father drove slowly through the gate, the bottom of the car scraping rocks each time the wheels rolled in and out of potholes. Annie pointed to the caragana hedge that ran parallel to the road, past the tall trees standing as sentries at the entrance. "That would be pretty in summer," she noted. The car stopped and we just sat.

Uncle Manuel saw the chicken house and reminded my mother that on the farm in North Dakota it was her job to collect the eggs and his job to wring the necks of the old chickens. He made screeching sounds and twirled his arm like a majorette with a chicken baton.

We then turned our attention to the large, wooden two-storey house, an impressive sight even though its dirty white walls were patched with asbestos shingles here and there. A wooden veranda swept across the front, forming wings that jutted past the corners of the house. Three bay windows on both storeys gave character to the front, like a face with enormous eyes.

Father knocked on the front door. The owner, Mrs. Rowe, slowly pulled it open. The inside was cavernous, simultaneously exuding charm and stuffiness. In the parlour, I was mesmerized by the three-level crystal chandelier that reflected the flames from the logs in the big stone fireplace. Red velvet drapes provided warmth and a *Gone with the Wind* atmosphere. A massive oak staircase swept elegantly to the second-floor balcony. Then the musty smell set off a chorus of coughing.

"Let's begin, shall we?" chirped Mrs. Rowe, moving to the foot of the stairs. We snaked in and out of the six rooms that ran off the upstairs balcony hall. Our eyes turned away from the bright sunlight streaming through the six-foot-high windows that graced some of the rooms.

Back on the main floor, Father saw the water pump beside the kitchen sink, a wood-burning stove, and an icebox. What shit! he thought.

"We'd need to rip a lot out," my mother whispered in his ear, as if reading his mind.

"We've done it before," he said.

"I'm going to tell you the history of this land," began Mrs. Rowe. "A farmer named Francis White applied for title to nearly 160 acres of land near the trail to Banff, on March 25, 1889." She told us that the Letters Patent arrived from England on 30 October 1890, granting free title to the land. With a mortgage of six hundred dollars, Francis White built a house and farmed until an old age. Then he sold nearly two-thirds of the acreage to John Charles Jackson, a rancher.

Jackson had lots of money-making ideas. He supplied Calgary's first settlers with eggs and raw milk, ladled out of a five-gallon can on the back of his horse-drawn cart. He concocted a scheme to subdivide the property into twenty-four parcels and a larger reserve area, which he registered for patent in August 1907. His plan was to develop the property, building houses in the Jackson Community.

Mrs. Rowe pulled a large roll from the drawer. "Here, look for yourselves. This is the map. The lots are labeled A to X. Here's my property, Block E." Her bony finger tapped the spot.

"Maybe you noticed the gun club? Here it is, Blocks J, K, L, M. Jackson's plan was not approved, so he began selling off the blocks. In October 1907, Charlotte and Daniel Vant Lewis bought this property. It took them five years to build this house. Daniel died in 1919. Probably the influenza. Two years later, Charlotte sold. It's passed through a few hands since then, but it's never been subdivided. Henry and I bought the place in '39."

My parents looked at each other—1939 was the year they had married. Father spoke up. "I think it's time to take a walk around the property." He put on his fedora and scooped me into his arms. "Let's go, Maria."

Our group moved along quickly. The house had a second entrance on the south side enclosed by a small veranda, and opposite this entrance was the chicken coop. We moved around the corner to the west side, where we saw the rickety back door of the house and, beside it, an old garage. A low-slung barn sat in a field of swaying grass to the west, its grey weathered planks dark and decrepit.

It didn't look like much of anything to me, but Gary's sharp eyes noticed something. "There aren't any doors on the barn! How can we keep animals?" he asked. Three large openings revealed stacks of baled hay.

"I think it's to store hay, not animals," Father answered.

Mother noticed a wilderness gully behind the garden. "We'd have to watch the kids closely," she cautioned.

"Look at this," said Uncle Manuel, "the water pump's taller than Gary."

Moving quickly, passing the cesspool, we came full circle back to the south side, stopping at the cellar. The two men brushed off the snow and lifted the flat door. The adults disappeared into the dark dirt cellar that housed a jagged black mountain of coal. They'd have to shovel coal into the ancient furnace every morning and night. We heard Father growl, "Shit!"

We got back in the car, and as we pulled away, Mother offered, "At least the property has electricity."

"Ya, but it'll take one heck of a lot of work," responded Manuel.

"Especially the kitchen," Father chimed in. "We'd be working hard seven days a week."

"There weren't any doors on the barn," repeated Gary and Marina in unison.

"No, but there are lots in the house. I counted twelve rooms," said Aunt Annie.

"Mommy, I feel sick." Mother

The old farmhouse, November 1951.

rolled down her window, drawing frigid air into the steamy car. I snuggled into her fur coat and slept.

Anxious to tell Gisetta about his discovery, my father hurried down the 4th Street hill as soon as we got home. As usual, Gisetta was in the kitchen. Sprinkling a mixture of meat and herbs on thin egg crepes, she rolled them like cigars and stacked the layers with tomato sauce. A priest or two from Our Lady of Perpetual Help Church across the street would be enjoying her stracci for dinner. After Ricardo's death and with her children grown, Gisetta's life centred on grandchildren, the church, and cooking.

My father kissed her soft cheek and peeled off his black leather gloves. He laid his overcoat across a chair, resting his grey fedora on top. Holding the tassels of his silk scarf out of the way, he flicked some meat filling into his mouth before sitting down at the table. "Marta and I found a villa. Near the southwest city limits. Can you imagine?"

Gisetta put aside the pan of stracci, wiped her hands, and sat down with her brother. "The place reminds me of the old Villa Mentuccia." He moved the sugar bowl to mark the location of the large house and ran his hands along the table circumference to indicate the three acres of land. Laying a pale yellow linen napkin in front of the sugar, he gave it the romantic title of "the courtyard." The salt shaker became the chicken house. Then he grabbed the grater off the counter and put it in the middle of the table—*ecco*, the barn.

"This is the place for my family and our future. We'll live upstairs above the restaurant."

They stared at the condiments.

"Why, Genesio? Why move so far from the Italian community? So far from your relatives, your friends, your patrons?"

"I need the space. The distance is good. In America, people are going crazy for nightclubs. My villa will be a nightclub, serving the best Italian food. People will drive the distance for the food. The spot is perfect. Adds to the mystique. It'll be harder for the police to patrol illegal drinking." Pointing at the tabletop, he continued. "See all the space? There'll be lots of room for parking. Gene's La Villa will be our home, too. The customers will be our guests. On Saturday night, they'll come out with their friends. They'll drink, dance, eat great food. The next day, they'll go for a Sunday drive to the country with the children. They'll all come to the villa—aunts, uncles, grandparents. I'll serve the kids spaghetti and meatballs. They'll run around with my kids. *Una grande famiglia.* One big family!"

"But what about Gene's Dine and Dance?" she asked.

"I want to get as far away from it as I can."

"But Riverside's been your home for nearly thirty years."

"What good is staying? Better to leave, take my name, start again."

"As long as the distance doesn't hurt our family."

"Never!"

"Stay for dinner. Phone Marta and tell her to bring the kids."

"If we get the place," said my father, "we'll own a villa. I feel like a pioneer. I've heard about the risks they took to open up the west, but I never thought that I'd be one of them."

My parents had spent the last six months investigating various options. They had even visited the Poscente family in Trail to explore refurbishing the MP (Mike Pistak) Hotel and its restaurant. Then they'd seen the dilapidated white house.

The priority the next morning was to call the real estate agent and discuss an offer. The cold reality was that nearly all their money remained tied up in Gene's Dine and Dance. Since Gene had walked away, Louis was running it.

"Mr. Cioni, your current home's a sure sell. The market's good." Calgary's population was booming, nearing

Gary and I play at the Riverside house before moving to La Villa, fall 1951.

The family tours the old farmhouse to determine if it should be purchased, November 1951. Left to right: Father, me, Uncle Manuel, Aunt Annie, and Mother.

130,000, and couples were looking for two-bedroom houses to start a family. "You'll probably get three thousand for it," remarked the agent. My parents had a few hundred dollars in Canada Savings Bonds and a few thousand dollars in the bank, but they'd need that for renovations.

"I have some good news, Mr. Cioni. Western Grain and Feed Company pays rent to Mrs. Rowe to store their hay in her barn. With the same agreement, you'll offset the mortgage costs."

"How about an offer of seven thousand dollars?" suggested my father. "With a mortgage."

"Mrs. Rowe's eager to sell and the Christmas holidays are around the corner. I'll write up the offer."

That New Year's Eve my father made a special dinner for my mother. Usually he refused to cook anything at home, but he felt that their morale needed a boost. Mrs. Rowe had refused their initial offer as too low. Then they saw the newspaper advertisements to celebrate New Year's Eve 1951 at Gene's Dine and Dance. "Look at the false advertising," Mother cried. They want your customers to think you're still there!" Their resolve to buy the villa grew stronger.

My mother set the table with their finest silver and china. Then she climbed on to a chair to lift down the wooden bluebird that they kept on top of the door frame. The little bird had come with the "Bluebird of Happiness" record that they bought when Jan Peerce, the Metropolitan Opera star, gave a concert at the Palace Theatre. The bluebird, with the family hopes and ambitions on its back, had become their phoenix rising. Tonight Martha wanted to remind Gene of that, so she placed the small bird in the middle of the table.

And when he sings to you,
Though you're deep in blue,
You will see a ray of light creep through …

They dressed for dinner, choosing outfits that were each other's favourites. My mother wore a rose-coloured satin dress and my father tucked his diamond stick pin into his silk tie. Frank Sinatra hits played in the background as they enjoyed the little feast, including Martha's favourite fried smelts and the traditional Antrodoco dish stracci, which Gene had lovingly prepared. When the clock struck midnight, Gene and Martha toasted the New Year with just one wish: to open La Villa in the spring.

They signed the deal on 8 January 1952. Gene and Martha Cioni were the owners of an $8,000 villa.

Eight

⤳ **THE SPIRIT** ⤳
OF PLACE

THE WAY THE PEOPLE
INHABIT THE PLACE
IS WHAT IS IMPORTANT.
THE ARCHITECTURE
SHOULD ENABLE
THE SPIRIT OF THE PLACE
TO BECOME REALITY.

—Christian Norberg-Schulz,
Genius Loci

WHEN NICK CORRADETTI saw Gene's villa, he let out a stream of dialect. "What a rotten shit hole! It all has to come down."

Gene nodded. "We need a bigger kitchen, a dining room, and an upstairs living space. I've got three thousand bucks. And I want to open La Villa before Easter."

"Jesus Christ! It's nearly the end of February. That's six weeks. Do you think I'm a magician?"

"I know you're going to build me the nicest supper club in Calgary. Simple. Elegant. Special."

"We'd better get to work then." Nick slapped his brother's back.

The crew of Antrodocani knocked out the walls dividing the first floor. Despite Aunt Annie's pleas, my father decided that the grand oak staircase had to go. "Space means more customers, and more customers mean more money," he had explained to her. Sixteen tables would fit in the new space. "It's about the same size as our last restaurant, Marta. Seventy customers, tops. Let's hope we have to make it bigger some day."

The only items that my parents had brought from Gene's Dine and Dance were the red and white checkered linen tablecloths, because they were home being laundered when Gene had walked out. The dining room decor would have to match. "I'd like to paint it the colours of the Italian flag," my father suggested.

"Okay, but modern tones," added Mother.

She watched Nick apply the first coat of Bordeaux-coloured paint to the bottom half of the dining room. "Stop! There's not enough light. I can't see if the colour's right."

"Damn it, Martha. It's only past three, do you want me to stop work now?"

"Do something else now, please. Leave the painting till tomorrow."

In the morning light, Nick painted the top half of the wall a mint green. "Well?"

"It looks good with the wine colour," Mother declared.

"Okay. I think we should put linoleum over the wood floors—," said Nick.

"I thought you might refinish them," Martha interrupted.

"Linoleum's easier to clean."

Mother chose dark green linoleum with veins of wine and cream from Nick's samples.

"Gene and I were thinking that the Wurlitzer would go where the old fireplace was."

"There's no room to dance," observed Nick.

"They'll twirl between the tables," my mother assured him.

In three weeks, Nick's crew had finished the dining room. It was simple, smart, and fifties cool, perfect for Gene's La Villa.

The old wallpaper was left in the living quarters. Nick built a basic kitchen with a small stove and fridge upstairs, where Mother could prepare breakfast and lunch for us. With the elegant staircase gone, there was only the servants' stairs connecting the two floors. These stairs were narrow and steep. Mother joked that the servants must have been either tiny adults or children.

My parents may have found the stairway claustrophobic, but I found jumping down the stairs ten at a time and bumping into the wall to stop irresistible. If my mother had caught me, she would have shouted, "*Ach te liber, God in himmel!*" She also would have taken away my dolls, but that only made the game more exciting.

Once the living quarters were ready, it was time for the most important job. My father stood near the kitchen entrance, shaking his head. "Nick, you know my customers like to watch me cook. They've got to be able to see the kitchen."

"How about I make a wider hall? Like a foyer. People will see into the kitchen as soon as they walk into the restaurant."

"A foyer, that's welcoming. I like it! Now, about my kitchen."

My father walked Nick through the room, pointing out where he wanted the stove, the fridge, the deep fryers, a preparation area. Gene dreamt about the details of his kitchen. Every day and every night, he walked around it, feeling the space change as Nick installed the new ceiling and the walls. The kitchen was large enough to accommodate an industrial-sized fridge, a six-burner stove, and two deep fryers, but on one walkabout, my father realized he'd need more light.

Nick went outside, poked around the snowbank, and returned. "Okay, Gene. I can push this outside wall out another six feet. If you want lots of light, I'll put a row of windows in the new wall. The cold will come in through the glass though."

"Don't worry. My kitchen is always steaming."

"I have an idea for this back entrance, too," added Nick. "We can make a loading dock. But with only three weeks left, I'm not sure I can finish it on time."

"Do it!" The chef continued to pace his semi-finished space. "I want stainless steel panels on the walls behind the appliances. Ya, I know it wasn't in my other kitchens, but I need it here. The wood in this house is old and dry. It would catch fire easily. Besides, it'll be easy to clean. And, Nick, while you're at it, put in a stainless ventilation hood."

Nick let out a long whistle. "It's going to be expensive."

"We'll save elsewhere. Oh, no linoleum in my kitchen, just wood. It helps my back. I'm going to order the appliances today. You can install them next week at the latest so I can get used to them before opening."

My parents and I drove downtown to the restaurant supply store. It was stocked with shelves of wonderful shiny things that Mother warned me not to touch. She ordered twelve dozen Medalta china place settings in white with a narrow dark green band, juice glasses, water tumblers, stainless cutlery, six dozen wooden-handled steak knives, and three dozen small, medium, and large oval serving platters.

While the order was being wrapped, I ran to find my father, who was at the back of the store picking up various blades and slashing the air. He settled on three for slicing, three for chopping, and six paring knives. Taking my hand, he led me to the pots—huge stainless steel beauties with thick bottoms. Even I was impressed. "Look." My father spotted a squat one for the spaghetti sauce, with large loop handles that fit his meaty fingers comfortably. It was solid and heavy and could hold forty-six quarts of sauce. It was perfect. He chose a twenty-quart stockpot for soup, three sauté pans, and four pots for boiling pasta. "Will you cook some spaghetti for me when we get home?" I asked.

"Maybe for dinner. It's only two."

Later, back at La Villa, Gene threw up his hands when he saw how much work was yet to be done. "Jesus, Nick! It's less than three weeks to opening. Where's the front entrance?"

"Relax, Gene. Tell me what you want outside."

"We need new stairs, wide ones. I've got an idea! Can you close in the porch so that customers will have a warm place to wait on cold nights? Ya know, while husbands bring the car or for people without reservations to wait."

"Good idea. Two sets of doors would keep the cold out of the dining room," Nick added. "I'll need to pick up more men—maybe another eight."

"Go ahead." Every morning, a growing pool of Italian newcomers gathered in Riverside, on the corner of 4th Street and 1st Avenue, in front of Luke's Drugstore. Nick would stop the next day and collect some to help finish La Villa.

Several men were assigned to build the new entrance and install floodlights. Four workers slapped coats of white paint over the dingy wooden siding. Others scaled the tallest ladders and crawled like ants over the roof, patching holes. They took advantage of every minute of the late March sunlight and used the new floodlights to work into the night. Nick brought in a bulldozer to clear the remaining snow and create a parking area the size of two football fields around the entrance. "Pick gravel that's large enough so that the stones don't get inside shoes," Gene advised.

Nick and his crew finished the renovation on 16 April. "God damn it! We made it!" said Nick proudly. "I didn't think we had a hope in hell of meeting your deadline."

Gene grabbed his larger brother in a bear hug. "Tell your gang that La Villa's first meal is for them. We'll have lunch at two." He made a pot of sauce and prepared polenta, the Antrodoco favourite, just as Zia Sofia had when he stayed in Trail, with pieces of succulent boiled pork spareribs pulled from the spaghetti sauce.

Gene brought out bottles of Chianti and filled the juice glasses for a toast. As the workers wiped their plates with crusty buns and helped themselves to salad, my father raised his glass. "To my brother and my *paesani, grazie* for making my villa restaurant. And doing it so fast!"

Sofia Poscente's Antrodoco Polenta

(from *Polenta on the Board* by Valerie Mitchell, courtesy the author)

(Serves 6–8)

16–18 c. (4–4.5 L) cold water

2 tsp. (10 mL) salt

4½ c. (1.1 L) coarsely ground cornmeal

2 tsp. (10 mL) butter

1½–2 c. (375–500 mL) spaghetti sauce (enough for 6–8 people)

1 c. (250 mL) each freshly grated Parmigiano and Romano cheeses

Put water and salt into a large heavy pot. Drizzle cornmeal into the water, stirring gently and constantly with a wooden spoon to prevent lumps from forming.

Turn the heat to high and continue stirring after all the cornmeal has been added. When the mixture starts to boil, adjust the temperature so that a steady gentle bubbling is maintained.

Continue stirring and cooking for 30 to 35 minutes or until the mixture is thick enough for the spoon to stand up in it for 3 to 4 seconds and the cornmeal grains have lost their grittiness. If it gets too thick early in the cooking process, add a little more water.

Stir in the butter, remove the pot from the stove, and pour the cooked polenta into the centre of an oiled wooden board. (Gene used large platters.) Immediately spread the hot polenta over the board (or platter) with a wooden spoon or spatula, to a thickness of 1 in. (2.5 cm).

Let the polenta sit for a few minutes to set, then ladle the sauce at regular intervals over the polenta. Gently spread the sauce to form a smooth layer over the polenta. Finish with a generous sprinkling of cheese.

When Nick finished the dining room and upstairs living space, my mother felt that her contribution to the remodeling of the new restaurant was done. With Gene concentrating on the kitchen, she could focus her energy on the search for staff. First though, they had to agree on how many staff were needed to do the job. "We can't afford more than a couple of waitresses," my mother suggested.

"We have to have good service. Customers are driving a long way and they'll want to be served as soon as they sit down," cautioned my father.

"Okay. Two during the week and an extra waitress on the weekend. If we're busy, we'll hire more."

"I need a reliable assistant to wash and chop vegetables and to assemble the anchovy salads. A dishwasher, too."

Mother placed an ad in the newspaper. Stella Volk arrived early for her interview, a petite, energetic Ukrainian woman with a lace hanky fanned and carefully pinned in the pocket of her suit jacket. Impressed by her neatness and punctuality, my mother described the job. "You'll start at 4:30 PM setting tables, filling salt and pepper shakers, sugar bowls. Once customers are seated, you'll fill water glasses, take orders, deliver dinners on trays, bring bills, and take the payment to the till. Above all, you must be pleasant and quick. During the week you'll finish around midnight. Friday and Saturdays, you'll stay until customers leave. It could be 3 AM. We'll send you home by taxi. On Sundays you can go home before 10 PM. Monday is your day off. We pay minimum wage, sixty cents an hour, but the tips are good."

"How good?" asked Stella

"Thirty, forty dollars a week. Maybe more than your salary. You may eat dinner here, free, of course."

Stella signed on. So did Kay Wiley. She was tall with short, dark hair and a demeanour that never ruffled. My mother could see that she and Stella would make a good team because each was confident and professional.

My father insisted that his kitchen staff must have previous experience; they had to pull their weight from the start. He interviewed Mary Regulski, who had worked in a restaurant in Europe. My father liked her energy and spunk. He described an anchovy salad and then asked her to prepare one, noting how long it took to clean the vegetables, chop, and then assemble the ingredients. When she automatically placed the anchovy diagonally across the top, he offered her the job.

"What would you do if I spilled a boiling pot of spaghetti?" My father asked Salina, another candidate.

"Check that no one is hurt badly, immediately put another pot of water on to boil, and then clean up." Salina got the job because she gave priority to replacing the order of spilled food. Ruby, an older woman, was hired as dishwasher.

With the staff in place, and the kitchen nearly completed, my parents discussed an opening date. "It has to be before May, that's when our money runs out," noted my mother, holding the bank statement in her hand. My father muttered, while looking at the Unico calendar. "How about April 26th? It's a Saturday and Saturday's are always good for business. Do you think we can be ready by then?"

"We'll have to do it." My mother hugged him.

All staff, including relatives, helped set up and stock La Villa for opening day. My mother decided that the foyer just outside the kitchen would be the administrative centre. From here she could keep one eye on the front door to welcome patrons and the other on the guests and waitresses in the dining room. The eyes in the back of her head watched out for Gary and me. She had the cash register placed here, as well as the family table, where she decided she would sit when she was on hostess duty. The black wall phone hung above the table, and my mother was relieved the instant it started ringing with people calling for information and directions. "Relax, Marta," my father said to calm her nerves. "Customers are looking forward to our opening and to eating good Italian food again."

Stella, the head waitress, directed what items—plates, glasses, silverware, and water jugs—should be put on the long shelves opposite the family table for easy access. Gary found a perfect spot under the counter for the large cardboard boxes of breadsticks, where he and I could pull out a handful as we passed by. Stella asked him to slide some crates of pop beside them, ready on demand. Then Gary had to crawl under the counter to plug in the till and the newly arrived Model Dairies freezer stocked with vanilla ice cream.

Meanwhile my father was directing his assistants how to set up the fridge while he stacked the twenty-pound boxes of Unico spaghetti, rigatoni, and linguine near the stove, with clearance for his fist to pull out an order. The assistants placed the bowls, graters, and pots for easy access. Nick had made a special wooden butcher's block with slots in the back for Gene's knives. He was sliding the knives into place as I passed by. "Where are you going?" he asked.

"Out of the way. Mummy told me to stay out of the way," I replied. My arms were loaded with dolls eager to move into their new house on the loading dock.

My father moved opening day up to Tuesday, 22 April 1952. I wore my pink party dress with a large, white satin ribbon tied in the front of my hair. Then my mother put on her olive brown checked suit with chocolate suede pumps. Gary was only twelve, but his shirt, tie, and serious expression made him seem more grown-up.

Mother had cooked dinner for the family. Gary and I ate while our parents drank coffee and smoked. Then Father asked Gary to get his piggy bank for the till float. Gary handed it over and watched as Father put a towel on top of the blue china pig and smashed it with a couple of whacks of the hammer. Gary winced, but he put the money into the various compartments of the cash register as Father had asked. "Don't worry. I'll give it back to you soon, with a bonus," he added, patting Gary's shoulder.

My father headed upstairs to dress. He teamed a new white shirt right out of the cellophane package with his favourite apron, the one he wore when he opened his first restaurant. After he rolled up the sleeves and smoothed his hair, he went down to his kitchen. He placed the bowls of black olives and anchovies beside the bottles of olive oil and red wine vinegar and put a pot of water on the stove to boil for the first order of spaghetti.

Each of us stood in one of the large dining room windows, eyes glued to the road, watching and waiting, minute after long minute. Dust! A car! A rattling car meant that it was old and heading to Rosscarrock, a little hamlet a couple of miles farther on.

Seven o'clock. At last, a car that didn't rattle. It slowed and turned off the road, pulling up to the new entrance. We were all outside now, smiling and waving.

"Congratulations!" Dr. Gelfand said, hugging my parents. "I'm starving after the long drive."

Arm in arm, Dr. Sid Gelfand and Chef Gene Cioni walked into La Villa, as though formally christening the place. They were entering the new and leaving behind the old—or so my father thought.

As Louis Carloni had threatened, he had taken legal measures to acquire Gene's name. On 12 October 1951, he and his nephew, Leo Fabbi, had signed legal agreements together to carry on business using the name "Gene's." Their actions effectively barred my father from calling his new restaurant Gene's La Villa. However, Harold Riley, our lawyer, had counselled that La Villa advertisements could use Gene's name as factual content. Mother created a new ad to run in the *Calgary Herald*.

The war for survival was on. When the ad for La Villa appeared, Louis countered by increasing his advertising, placing two ads at a time in the Saturday newspaper:

Announcing
The Opening of
La VILLA
Appetizing Food in a Country Atmosphere
by
Gene Cioni formerly of
GENE'S DINE & DANCE
Specializing in
GENE'S SPAGHETTI — RAVIOLI → FRIED CHICKEN — STEAKS.
Open 5 p.m. to 3 a.m. Weekdays
Sundays 5 p.m. to 10 p.m.
CLOSED ON MONDAYS
Gene looks forward to again serving his many friends and former patrons.
Located at 1220 - 33rd Street S.W., Opposite the West End of the Municipal Golf Course, 2 Blocks North of the Gun Club.
PHONE 45644

★★ **NOTICE** ★★
There is only ONE
GENE'S DINE & DANCE
in Calgary — 109 - 4th St. N.E.
Gene's Dine and Dance is in no way associated with any other restaurant in the City.

NOTICE — There is Only ONE in Calgary
Calgary's Original
ITALIAN CUISINE
Gene's
FAMOUS FOR GOOD WHOLESOME FOOD
Hours: Supper Hours:
5 p.m. to 3 a.m.   5 p.m. to 8 p.m.
ORDERS PREPARED TO TAKE OUT
NOTICE — Gene's will remain closed Sundays
For Banquets, Wedding Receptions, Club Dinners, Etc.
PHONE 25115 FOR YOUR RESERVATION
109 - 4th St. N. E. — One Address Only — 25115

The newspaper inadvertently became the battlefield for competing ads that often appeared on the same page. Former customers wanted to be with Gene; they'd been waiting to eat his food again and to enjoy the spirit of the place that he and my mother created. It took only one dinner in Riverside for customers to know that my father wasn't there. "Where's Gene?" they would ask. Some patrons revelled in telling my parents of the lengths to which Louis went to avoid answering, but eventually there was a standard reply, "Gene's off tonight."

My father would have been astounded to know that Louis was also using his name in another way. On 17 November 1952, Louis had officially incorporated Gene's Spaghetti Society,

Restaurant family in the kitchen, 1953.

operating at the Riverside restaurant. The initial board of directors comprised Louis and Leo Fabbi; six others in the Italian community also signed the document. Among the listed "objects" of this society were "to provide for the recreation of the members, to acquire land and erect buildings, to encourage amateur games, to provide a meeting place for the discussion of questions affecting the interests of the community, to procure the delivery of lectures and to arrange musical and dramatic entertainment, to establish a library, and to provide a centre and suitable meeting place for the various activities of the community." It may be that Gene's Spaghetti Society and its objects were the precursor to what is now the Calgary Italian Club.

Although he formed Gene's Spaghetti Society, Louis's main goal was still to crush La Villa and its owner. But after several months, my father struck the decisive blow. Following Harold Riley's advice, he placed his photo in his La Villa advertisements. There, for all to see, smiling in his formal white chef's hat and bow tie, was "Gene Cioni, originator of Calgary's Italian Cuisines." In December 1953, the Riverside charade crumbled—Louis closed Gene's Dine and Dance and took down the sign.

Since opening, the spirit of La Villa grew steadily. On a warm June afternoon in 1952, the Goodings went for their ritual Sunday drive, intent on finding that new restaurant their friends couldn't stop talking about. They had been warned about the gravel road, and as they bounced along with open windows, the dust clouds made them cough. Passing the sign for the Calgary Gun Club, Doris squinted at her scribbled directions and said that they were almost there.

A large white house came into view, but there was no sign. "Do you think this house is it?" she asked, as Hal pulled into the gravel yard. They sat for a few minutes looking the place over. "Let's go in," Doris said, untying her aqua chiffon head scarf and plumping her hair.

"Wait! Don't get out!" her husband cautioned. "There's no sign. It could be a roadhouse!" Doris retied her scarf as the tires spit gravel.

A month later, they joined a group of their friends for a night out at the fabulous new restaurant that they had been unable to find. Now they saw that a large neon sign had been installed at the gate of the big white house. Sitting atop a twelve-foot steel pole, the white glow of "Gene's La Villa" was a beacon for the cognoscenti. My mother had been uneasy about spending two hundred dollars, but when Gene looked up and saw his name in lights, he thought, It's worth every penny.

Family portrait, fall 1952.

Nine

**FAMILY LIFE
AT LA VILLA**

HOME IS WHEREVER THE
FAMILY IS TOGETHER.

—Martha Cioni

"THESE BEDROOM windows are too dangerous!" Mother said. Six-foot-high glass soared from the low sill. "The children could fall out!"

"Have someone fix it," Gene said, heading downstairs. He was pre-occupied with finishing his kitchen on time. Besides, he remembered that the windows in his old house in Antrodoco had been just as large, but no one thought twice about them. In any case, he relied on Martha to handle such matters. Their different temperaments made them an effective team.

Mother felt a twinge of regret that the family had migrated so far from the relatives, friends, and homes of Riverside, where windows were family-friendly. She asked Nick to make three window jambs and then, summoning my brother and me, instructed in her sternest voice, "Don't go close to the windows. You might fall out." Whether spurred by the warning, lured by the glass space, or perhaps a desire to escape the isolation, I was drawn nose-to-pane to imagine the thrill of a straight twenty-foot splat to the gravel.

Gary was twelve when La Villa, like an asteroid, shattered his comfortable world. We had moved into La Villa in February 1952, as soon as the upstairs renovation was completed. My parents had decided that Gary would remain in St. Angela's, in Riverside, to finish grade seven. He'd stay at Auntie Gisetta's during the week and return home for the weekend; otherwise, it would be an hour-and-a-half trek each way to and from school. Gary was adamant: "I want to stay with my family."

"He'll get used to it," Father advised, conveniently forgetting his own pangs of loneliness as a young boy in Antrodoco, and even years later during a visit to Vancouver. So strong had been his yearning for his family that he phoned and begged, "Marta, please bring Gary and join me. Take the train this afternoon and I'll meet you tomorrow at the station."

Each Sunday night, Mother gave Gary the same pep talk. "This way is so much easier. Before you know it, it'll be Friday." But Gary was his father's son. When the teachers reported that his grades were sliding, Mother had to accept that the plan wasn't working. On a Friday in March, she took Gary's hand and said, "Let's go home. Home is wherever the family is together. And we'll be together at La Villa."

After that, every school morning at 5:30, my mother pulled on pants and a coat over her nightgown and stuffed the trouser legs into boots. She took a flashlight, unbolted the main door, and walked quickly outside to the cellar, where she descended into the frozen earth to clear out the ashes from the furnace and shovel in coal to make a blazing fire.

Gary got up at 6:00 and was able to dress in a warm room. By now, Mother was cooking his porridge, and the smell brought me to the table, too. She made cinnamon toast and large mugs of Ovaltine, my favourite. After breakfast, Gary struggled with his load of winter gear. He had a new navy blue hat with fur lining and big ear flaps. I liked his old raccoon hat better. He used to swish the long tail to wave goodbye to me, but now Mother said it wasn't warm enough for the trek. With his leather book bag across his shoulders, he crossed the parking lot. At the edge of the floodlights, he turned and waved to us as we watched from the window, then he disappeared into the early morning blackness.

My mother cleared the breakfast dishes and then we slipped into my bed for a morning nap. By late morning, Father awoke to shovel more coal and to prepare his shopping list for the day. Mother always added what she needed for the family dinner. She believed that it was important that we eat together as a family, so she cooked dinner Tuesday through Saturday.

We ate an early family dinner in the dining room, in order to finish by the time the customers arrived. Gary always chose Father's soup and anchovy salad as a starter to Mother's meat and vegetables main course; I preferred to add Father's spaghetti at the end. "Wait until I cook the next spaghetti order," he instructed me. "I'll put a little extra for you."

My father and I had formed a special bond when I was three, a "spaghetti tie," we called it. We were on vacation in Coeur d'Alene, Idaho. As was his custom, Father toured the town, looking for a restaurant that offered spaghetti. We'd go there for lunch and he'd order one serving. His test was simple: if the spaghetti was cooked *al dente*, and if the sauce tasted of fresh tomatoes and herbs rather than homogenized tomato soup, he'd willingly try other menu items.

At one restaurant, the waiter brought the plate of spaghetti, and my father served each of us a few strands. I chewed and then spat it out. "You call this spaghetti!" I wailed. Scooping me into his arms, my proud father cried, "*Che piccolina*! That's my baby, she knows good spaghetti."

After dinner, Gary would settle himself at the family table and, turning on the radio, begin his homework. Mother insisted that his school work come before any restaurant chores that Father might assign. Staff cleared the dishes and Mother went upstairs to dress for work.

As the hostess, she'd assembled a wardrobe of suits and tailored dresses, usually with three-quarter-length sleeves and a wide belt to emphasize her small waist. On days when I wasn't hungry for after-dinner spaghetti, I would lie on the bed and watch her. I followed the thin black line down the back of her silk stockings to see what

The Spaghetti Tie, La Villa kitchen, c. 1953. Left to right: Ruby, Mary, Salina, Gene, Gary, and me.

colour of pumps she had chosen. My favourites were made of suede. I watched her take a large powder-puff from the pink glass jar to dab her face, and from a gold case she applied rouge in circles on her porcelain cheeks. She'd select a shade of red lipstick to match her outfit, fill in her slender bowed lips, and put a tissue between them to blot the excess. Next she'd tuck her wispy brown hair behind her ears with tortoise-shell combs. From the red velvet box with the little pearls glued on the lid, she'd pick clip-on earrings and either a brooch or her single strand of cultured pearls. She always wore her engagement present from my father, the small gold wristwatch with tear-shaped rubies holding the face. Now came my favourite part; my mother reached for the midnight blue bottle and dabbed a few drops of Evening in Paris perfume behind her ears and on her wrists. Then she hugged me.

Days at La Villa seemed to drag on forever. With Gary at school and my parents busy at the restaurant, I had no one to play with but the cats. So I was ecstatic when, at the age of four, I was allowed to go grocery shopping with my father. Together, we went to Safeway to buy meat and to pick an apple for me, and then popped by the bakery next door to pick up whole wheat bread for breakfast. The lady there always gave me a cookie. Sometimes we stopped at LoVecchio's Fruit & Groceries near 14th Street, where my father would visit with Joe and Lena LoVecchio.

Mary Comella, one of the other owners, knew that I was fascinated with the cash register so she taught me how to operate it. But what good is a cash register without customers? Mary took care of that too by cajoling her nephew, Sal, into the game. Sal filled a shopping cart and lined up lemons, peppers, celery, and a couple of onions. Under Mary's watchful eye, I'd ring up the sale and take his imaginary money. "Thank you for shopping at LoVecchio's," I'd say. Rolling his eyes, Sal would put everything back in the cart for restocking.

After a hot beef sandwich at Jimmie's Restaurant, my father was ready to tackle the 17th Avenue hill. It was a personal challenge to see what speed he could reach by the time he got to the Tecumseh naval barracks at the top. Thirty miles over the speed limit was just a start. Inevitably, a police car was waiting at the top of the hill. "Gene Cioni, slow down," the policeman boomed over the loudspeaker. My father flattened the gas pedal. "Hold on, honey. We'll beat 'em home."

By the time the police arrived at La Villa, my father had already unloaded the car. "Damn it, Gene. You have to slow down."

My father's response was always the same: "Come in and have something to eat."

Summer was a more relaxed time for our family. When school ended, my father dropped Gary off at one of his favourite places, Jaffe's Books, on 8th Avenue between 1st and 2nd Streets East. As a frequent customer, Gary received special attention from Mr. Jaffe. "Ah, you've come for your summer supply." The owner smiled and led my brother to the back of the long, narrow store. There, he opened a trap door in the floor and turned on the light. "Watch the stairs. Call if you need help."

All afternoon, Gary wandered through the subterranean labyrinth of small rooms under 8th Avenue, browsing the thousands of books. He searched for boys' books on World War II, finding several of the Biggles series about a British war hero. Then he selected some Andy Hardy, a perennial favourite, and a classic or two, like *The Lone Ranger*. Leaving his favourite genre to the end, he finally unearthed dozens of mysteries. Hauling four boxes of treasure to the cash register, my brother phoned home and waited for a ride. Father glanced at the boxes, pulled out his wad of bills, and, with a twinkle of pride,

Father having a snack while I visit him, 1955.

paid for his son's summer entertainment. Mr. Jaffe patted Gary on the shoulder. "Enjoy the summer. I'll stock up for your next visit."

When Gary wasn't "reading out the polio scare," as he called it, he and I vied for the honour of accompanying Father on his shopping rounds. Nearly a teenager, Gary was big enough to help carry the heavy boxes. I wasn't really able to help; nevertheless, I began to resent Gary's role as summer shopping assistant. One morning I was looking out a big window and saw the two of them getting into the car as though they were sneaking out. I ran to my mother. "It's my turn," I sobbed.

"Maybe next time."

I began to bang on the window to catch their attention.

"Maria, stop pounding the window. Get away from there," ordered my mother. "Right now!" My fist went through the glass, slicing my wrist and releasing a fountain of blood. I was strangely quiet as Mother carefully pulled my hand out, trying to avoid the shards. She wrapped it in a towel, applying pressure. I could see the fear in her eyes and her lips holding back rebuke. She phoned for an ambulance, hoping that they'd travel this far. By the time it arrived, however, the bleeding had stopped. The paramedics said that stitches weren't necessary, so my relieved mother made them a cup of coffee for their efforts. Initially, my father was angry with me because I had hurt myself, and then he softened. "You can shop with me on Tuesdays as long as you are good on all the other days."

Mother was constantly warning me to be careful. "Don't run in the restaurant" became part of the background noise. Running through the kitchen one evening in 1955, I collided with a cauldron of boiling coffee. Hearing my screams, Mother ran to me. Ripping the steaming clothes from my body, she could see places without skin. She drizzled some cool water over my chest, then gingerly laid a silk scarf on top and sat with me until I eventually fell asleep. By morning I was covered with blisters from my waist to my neck. "We've got to get Maria to the hospital," Mother announced, as my father was having a late-morning coffee with visiting police friends.

"We'll take her in the cruiser," offered Sergeant Percy Weyman and his partner. Mother and I sat in the back and we were off. The siren that blasted cars off the road was a welcome distraction, but they weren't driving as fast as my father. An emergency room doctor declared that I had first-degree burns and after dressing them advised that I would have to go to a doctor for several weeks to have my bandages changed regularly. The advice to my shaken mother was "Call your doctor. He'll tell you what to do." More cars were blasted aside on our way home to La Villa.

My chest was so painful that I couldn't rest and I had trouble breathing. I didn't even want spaghetti. As Fortuna would have it, Sid Gelfand came in for dinner that night. "Doc, we had an accident," began Father, and then filled in the details.

Soon the soft-spoken man with the gentle hands was rewinding my tensor bandage. "There you go," he said, patting my head. "You'll find it easier to breathe now." He turned to my anxious parents. "It was too tight, cutting off her circulation. Bring her to the office in a couple days."

Gary read me a story and Father said, "We'll listen to music tomorrow." I listened over and over again to "Eh Cumpari" sung by Julius La Rosa.

For half of my eighth year, I saw Dr. Gelfand weekly. I hadn't gone to the doctor very often till then, so I was nervous. Dr. Gelfand's calm, gentle demeanour put me at ease until he started pulling off the tape that held my dressing in place. The pain made me cry, and seeing the bright red skin with yellow mounds on my chest made me queasy. "You're very brave," Dr. Gelfand told me, attempting to instill courage. Once I knew what was coming, it didn't seem to hurt as much, and gradually the bandages got smaller. I actually looked forward to seeing Dr. Gelfand until one day he said, "You're done, young lady. And when you're a big girl, I promise there won't be any scars."

The space and the freedom that I experienced once we moved to La Villa led me to believe that I was now a big girl. In the early evening, I shifted my playground into the dining room, where I learned that I could be entertained by sitting and talking to customers who were family friends. Over the years, their children became my playmates at Sunday dinners as we gathered around the jukebox. I delighted in teasing the shy boys "to come and dance."

Dancing became my passion as I whirled the daytime hours away waiting for Gary to get home from school. I had the jukebox pumping out songs as though it was a radio, and soon I knew the lyrics to hundreds of songs. By the age of five, I fantasized that La Villa customers were coming to see me perform. I gave a pretty good five-minute song and dance show but got the hook from my parents when they realized that my ambition was growing, not tiring. But I was multi-talented; if I couldn't perform I would find another way to attract attention. My parents must have enjoyed the calm, and they certainly weren't ready for the storm. "What are you doing?" asked my father as I came into the dining room one day with paper and scotch tape.

"I'm going to have an art show for the customers," I informed him as I began to paste my drawings to walls.

My father chuckled and made the error of saying, "I'll buy a few of your paintings." The light went on: if he would buy them then certainly the customers would as well. Mother came to stop the nonsense, but she was too late. By this time, Lynne and Swede Hanson had come in for dinner and offered to buy some of my work. As I sat with the Hansons, Mother removed my artistry from the walls. Lynne took pity on me and invited me to spend a day with her and her son, John, at her house. I had learned my lesson: don't bother the customers too much and, if you are cute enough, they'll play with you.

From then on, I went for spins in the Ramas's Cadillac convertible, sitting on the armrest between them. I was a guest at the gun club, and I practised ballet at the Hansons' house. I still occasionally trolled the dining room in the early evening, teaching customers the proper way to twirl spaghetti on their forks. One night, Firpo Zbyszko, a massive, bald wrestler, allowed me to touch his thick black, waxed handlebar moustache.

La Villa was closed on Mondays, except for the occasional private party and my father's annual Holy Name Spaghetti Dinner fundraiser for our parish church. When my cousin Marina married, my parents offered to host the wedding reception as long as it was on a Monday. Normally though, Monday was my parents' day of rest. They picked Gary and me up after school to go home and get dressed for dinner. Three Mondays out of four, we ate at the Palliser Hotel. We donned our Sunday clothes, complete with gold jewellery and gloves, ready to enter the marble lobby of the CPR hotel. Friends at the bellhop station and the newspaper kiosk greeted us. The waitress, Dorothy Garshman, stood in the oak-panelled dining room with outstretched arms ready to hug Gary and me. Her warmth, jokes, and stories made going to the Palliser fun for us both. I'm sure that the hotel brought back memories for my father. He had worked as a busboy in this very dining room in the late 1920s. Now he sat with his wife and children at his usual table near the blazing logs in the stone fireplace.

Our restaurant family didn't use menus. The chef came out to greet us and to recommend the evening's best. My parents ordered medium-rare prime rib of beef with Yorkshire pudding, or sometimes roast lamb or pork. Dorothy always took Gary into the kitchen to choose whatever he wanted, which was usually some of everything, swimming in rich brown gravy. I ate two courses, onion soup and then Yorkshire pudding and gravy. To me, the large windows that fronted the railway tracks were far more interesting than the food. I watched the conductors, porters, and passengers weaving along the platform and could hardly wait for the trains to start moving. The motion of the massive engines shook the ground, causing a tinkling of crystal to ripple across the dining room.

Although I loved seeing our friends and watching the trains, I have to admit that the hotel wasn't my favourite place to eat. I much preferred going to Linda Mae's for Chinese food, because rather than eating one dish, we'd share them all. We would go there once a month for an early dinner so that we could also take in a seven o'clock movie. As soon as the waiter brought the small bowls of soy sauce and sesame seeds, Gary and I jockeyed to wet our forks in the soy sauce so that the sesame seeds would stick. Eating the salty, crunchy treat off the fork tines was a fun start to the meal. While other customers browsed the menu, my father was in the kitchen with the cook, selecting our dinner items: wonton soup for Gary, barbecued spareribs for my mother, sweet and sour chicken for me, and chow mein for my father. The food came quickly and we gobbled it down so that we could get to the movie on time. Without question, Father's favourite movies were Italian, but he also enjoyed American films featuring Italian stars such as Mario Lanza, Dean Martin, and Gina Lollobrigida, as well as Jan Peerce, the Jewish opera singer. He thought that Dean Martin's sidekick, Jerry Lewis, was hilarious.

When Gary was about seven, Father began to take him along to see the latest Italian films from post-war Italy. He so wanted to teach Gary about "his" country that he didn't think about whether or not the content was appropriate for my brother's age. Gary was frightened by scenes in the war-ravaged streets of Roberto Rossellini's *Rome, Open City* and had nightmares, but he was enchanted with the search of a father and son in Vittorio De Sica's *The Bicycle Thief*. Gary's teenage interest in the opposite sex was stoked by the voluptuous Silvana Mangano's suggestive dance in *Bitter Rice* and Anna Magnani's earthy performance in *The Golden Coach*.

Our family loved movies, so when my father announced, "We're going to buy one of the first televisions in Calgary!" we thought we

Gary and I beside the newest member of the family, the Crosley TV set, November 1954.

were getting our own mini-theatre. One channel, CHCT-TV, beamed into our living room on 12 October 1954, and before Friday dinner we gathered around the nineteen-inch, blond wood, Crosley black and white TV set, which Hy Belzberg had arranged to be specially delivered and installed in our upstairs living room. My mother had reorganized the room, placing a lime green, gooseneck floor lamp behind the set for proper lighting, as the newspaper articles advised. We watched the news and the *Red Buttons Show*. Fidgeting in his armchair, my father asked, "Where're the movies?"

Checking the four-hour schedule in the newspaper, my mother responded, "Just in the theatres."

While my father looked forward to going to movies at least once a month, I had to wait patiently for a year for my favourite event, my birthday party. My seventh birthday party was held at La Villa on a Monday. It was the first time that most of my grade two friends had been to a restaurant, so they dressed in their best party dresses and black patent shoes for the occasion. About a dozen of us took over the dining room and the dance floor. Since the Wurlitzer was new to them, I shoved a handful of quarters that Mother had given me in the slot and demonstrated how to punch in the number associated with a song. I also taught my friends how to twirl spaghetti, holding a forkful against a spoon. As soon as the Crew Cuts finished "Sh-Boom," Mother carried out the birthday cake. She always made my favourite angel food cake without icing, but she decorated it in another way. "Hey, there's money in my cake!" shouted the guests as they discovered quarters wrapped in foil.

By eight o'clock, the party had ended and several guests were crammed into our car for a ride home. I scrunched beside my father. The girls were still excited and boisterously distracting. "Girls, please be more quiet," my father asked as he tried to concentrate on finding their houses.

Then from the back seat I heard a low voice, "Who does he think he is? He can't even speak English." I turned and gave her a drop-dead stare—she was definitely off next year's party list. I wondered if my father had heard, but he just drove on.

When we were alone in the car going home, I asked him about it. "Yes, I heard," he said. "But I didn't say anything because I didn't want to embarrass her any more than she had already embarrassed herself. Maybe at school tomorrow you'll talk to her. Tell her I'm Canadian just like her."

After my birthday, my next favourite celebration was Christmas Eve with all my cousins and Auntie Gisetta's once-a-year specialties. My father closed the restaurant on Christmas Eve and Christmas Day so we could be with Gisetta and her children, their families, and a few friends—more than thirty people—to enjoy Gisetta's Antrodoco specialties. We sat for hours nibbling on the ten-course, traditional meatless dinner. Both Gary and I were avowed fish-haters, but I happily ate the baccala and prunes in tomato sauce until, years later, I realized that it was salt cod. My parents dove into the deep-fried, batter-dipped smelts and fish fritters. At midnight Mass at Our Lady of Perpetual Help Church, Gisetta and Genesio looked at their families occupying two rows of pews and smiled contentedly.

We celebrated the main holidays at Auntie Gisetta's and Sunday dinners at La Villa. Gisetta's daughters Connie and Jean and Jean's family were included in this Sunday tradition. I remember watching impatiently for their arrival one Sunday afternoon. "Mommy, the Amanteas are here!" I screamed, heading for the parking lot just as my three cousins, dressed in identical outfits, bounded from the car. Jackie, the eldest, spent a lot of time with me at La Villa and was like a little sister. I admired her for her daredevil stunts. At three years old, she climbed the six-foot-high tower of pop cases. Reluctantly, I had to squeal on her when she froze at the top.

Meanwhile, my father helped Gisetta out of the back seat and squired her to the family table. For a good part of the afternoon, they sipped tea and talked about the new Italians. "I can't understand why the Canadian embassy keeps telling people there are plenty of jobs in Calgary," Gisetta started.

"Ya, Marta read that after Ontario and Quebec, Alberta gets the most immigrants."

"Immigrants can't find jobs. Imagine, the Salvation Army's set up a soup kitchen to help hundreds of them make it through winter. What a shame!" Gisetta shook her head. Then, shifting in the chair as though making room for another thought, she continued, "Some officials from downtown were at church the other day. They said our community has had the most success helping newcomers fit in. In a year, in 1955, they're going to open an Immigration Reception Centre. It'll be the first in Canada, and the Canadian government's paying for it."

Jack Amantea was uncharacteristically glum as he joined the conversation. "You have to help me out, Gene," he pleaded. The previous Monday my father had spotted a magnificently crafted little feather bird sitting on a perch in a gilded cage in the window of Reed's China & Giftware, across the street from Amantea Shoes. He'd run to get Jack. "Look at this! It's like the bluebird of happiness. Look, I'll wind it up." The head and delicate beak moved as the little bird sang. The tail fluttered and the bird could sing a melody. "What do you think?" Before Jack could answer, my father had already turned to the salesperson. "How much?"

"Just $150."

"Let me speak to the owner."

Shaking hands, my father introduced himself and Jack. "How many birds do you have?"

"The only two in Calgary."

"We'll give you two hundred dollars cash for the two."

Putting his hand on Jack's shoulder, my father reassured him, "It's like the bluebird of happiness. It'll bring us *fortuna*. We'll have the only two in town. They're beautiful and a good deal. Come on, I'll loan you the money."

"Sold!" said the owner.

Now Jack told the rest of the story. "My wife was furious when she heard the price of that bird. Jean said I was taking food from our babies' mouths, and she hasn't spoken to me since."

Father leaned closer. "Don't worry! Enjoy the bird! Take time to pay me back. Take five years if you want. Remember, it's good luck—it's the bluebird of happiness!" Later in the afternoon my father spoke with Jean and assured her that he had paid for the bird, not Jack.

Sometimes my mother's family came for Sunday dinner as well. Uncle Manuel, Aunt Annie, and my teenage cousin Marina took the bus to the end of the line and phoned for a ride. Gary and Marina usually found a quiet space to read comics until Father summoned them to grate the cheese. Three or four tables were put together to accommodate both sides of the family. Just like customers, we sat at tables covered with red and white checkered tablecloths, and the staff served us a full-course dinner that was finished around five.

Many customers brought their families to enjoy an early Sunday dinner at La Villa. Some came directly from the Calgary Gun Club, a half mile south of the restaurant. Farmers and business people alike belonged to the club, lured by its low membership fees and a "bring your own rifle" policy. They stood elbow to elbow with newly arrived Americans, shooting clay discs. This was mainly a man's sport with a notable exception—Vera Holdsworth. One Sunday, this champion shooter decided to take her family to the new Italian restaurant she'd heard so much about. Vera brought her young son, Ron, daughter Maureen, and her mother, Mary Harris.

Martha seated the family, and Gene was soon introducing himself. "We've come from the gun club"—Vera smiled, shaking hands—"It's our first visit. What do you suggest?" They settled on spaghetti and meatballs for the kids, chicken cacciatore for Mary, and ravioli with veal for Vera.

Placing a cup of breadsticks on their table, my mother offered, "Perhaps your children would like to join mine. My son's putting money in the Wurlitzer. That's my daughter, Maria, sliding on the dance floor." Vera asked when the restaurant had opened, where Martha and Gene had come from.

Mary Harris joined in. "My husband and I started a business, Harris Health Wondro Tonic. So I know what it's like to raise a family and to work."

By six, there was a rush of families into the dining room, and Vera recognized many of them. As the Hansons passed, Lynne stopped. "Hello, Vera, I'm so glad you took our advice. We were just here last night. Our son Johnny wanted spaghetti, so here we are again!"

"It's like a party," observed Mary.

"More like one big family," added Vera.

As they were getting ready for bed that night, my mother commented on how much she had liked Mary and her family. "I'd like to be friends with her. It's funny, but I see more of our customers than I do of our old friends."

"I know," my father replied, climbing into bed. "Maybe in a few months we'll have a party and invite our old friends and new customer friends."

My mother and Mary Harris became friends, just as my mother had predicted. Mary was seventy years old, a cousin of film director John Huston. She'd come to Calgary from Ireland as a young girl. My mother was more than a little surprised to hear the stately old lady confide, "I adore watching wrestling on television even though Vera disapproves. I'd love to go to a match but she'd be horrified." Stu Hart, the wrestling promoter, had invited Gene and Gary to the big Friday night event, so Mother asked Mary if she'd like to go along. Mary quickly agreed.

Father and Gary picked up Mary, and soon they were settled into the ringside seats. They were so close to the action that they could feel the flecks of sweat. A few times they even had to duck as bodies flew over the ropes. When the evening was over, my father suggested that they link arms to stay together in the crowd. Suddenly their path was blocked by a young woman staring in disbelief. "Grandma, what are you doing here?" demanded a shocked Maureen Holdsworth.

"What are YOU doing here?" Mary shot back. "Tell you what. If you don't tell your mother that I was here, I won't tell her that you were."

"A deal, Grandma!"

Gene's La Villa was a sophisticated restaurant, patronized by many of Calgary's most prominent citizens like the Holdsworth family; however, my father still had a romantic notion of it as a farm. Determined to raise chickens, he gave Gary the job of feeding them. My brother went one step further and trained the biggest bird, whom he named Fred, to eat from his hand and walk on a string leash. He didn't bother telling my parents about his pet, not even one Saturday, when he noticed that Fred was missing from his pen. The next day at

Sunday dinner, Gary was regaling his cousins with stories of the talented bird and sighed, "Fred's gone."

Hearing his son as he set the platter of roast chicken on the table, my father said, "Who's Fred?" Gary looked at my father and then at the bird. "We're eating Fred!" he cried.

At La Villa, I found my first playmates hiding under the stairs at the kitchen door. Angela the cat and her continual broods of rainbow kittens joined my tea parties. A few of the kittens, knowing no better, ended up in doll clothes. For me, these feline playmates were more fun than our old grey Persian cat, who Gary said hated La Villa so much that he walked back to Riverside several times.

My father also found a pet, a stray border collie that came to feast on La Villa scraps. He named the little black dog with white feet Boots. When Father was busy, Boots joined my make-believe world to ride in a doll carriage or fetched balls with Gary; otherwise, he was dashing after birds and patrolling the parking lot. My father had given permission to the neighbouring Jacques' Ranch to cut across La Villa land a couple of times a year when the cowhands moved hundreds of head of cattle to different pastures. Boots was alerted by the distant sound of pounding hooves, and when the herd came onto our property, he took off to run roughshod around them. "Quick,

Angela the cat and me, fall 1953.

In the kitchen, c. 1954. Left to right: Jenny, Fire Officer Lew Marks, Mother, and Mary.

come look at Boots!" called my father. We caught glimpses of him circling as the dust cloud grew huge, seeing him trip and roll through the high grass, his piercing bark hurrying the rumbling animals away.

My father loved Boots's courage and big heart, so when the dog disappeared, he was very concerned. We searched everywhere, and Father put out more food, but he was nowhere to be seen. The days passed and our fears grew. One afternoon a week later, a car swung into La Villa's parking lot, skidding on the gravel as it screeched to a halt. I was playing on the loading dock and heard the noise. My parents came outside—they had heard it, too. The driver got out and opened the back door. Boots shot out and jumped into my arms. My mother walked towards the woman to speak to her, but immediately she jumped back in the car. Mother realized that this wasn't Boots's rescuer, it was his kidnapper. Mother ran towards the car shouting, "Thief, coward. Come back!" but it was too late, the car roared off. My father petted Boots and said, "I think that this little dog gave that old cow a hard time."

La Villa was not a safe place for animals, but my mother's biggest fear was that it might also be dangerous for us. She awoke one morning to the smell of smoke. Controlling her panic, she followed the trail downstairs to the restaurant kitchen. She looked everywhere. Finding nothing, she woke my father. "Can you smell smoke?" Moving closer to his face, she said again, "Can you smell smoke?"

Gene took a big whiff. "Yes," he said. She called the fire department and soon a crew lumbered through the restaurant. Nothing. My father began his routine. Heaving his forty-six-quart stainless steel pot onto the stove, he soon had the tomato sauce simmering and began preparing the meatballs.

"Gene, the smoke smell is stronger."

"Relax," Father replied, "it's the pot on the burner."

No sooner had they spoken when Lew Marks, the fire prevention officer, walked in, following up on his crew's earlier visit. He smelled smoke. The experienced nostrils followed the wall, stopping beside the stove. With the back of his axe, he tapped the plaster just below the steel sheeting. A giant fireball flew out of the wall. "Stand back!" he shouted, but Father had already bolted. Apron in hands, he grabbed the pot handles. With a roar of superhuman strength, he lifted his precious tomato sauce and raced for the safety of the dining room. Marks was a quick thinker, too. He grabbed the fire extinguisher and enlisted Mother to fill pots with water.

By the time my father returned to the kitchen, the fireman was standing by the charred wall, sweat pouring down him. With a hand on Marks's shoulder, Gene asked, "Can I open tonight?"

Pass the Bucket, Student, Please!

Here's one way to bring the message home!

Fire Prevention Bureau Officer Lew Marks has been pounding fire prevention at Calgarians for almost four years through every medium possible.

Monday he discarded his booklets, movies and prepared speeches and found himself an actual fire to prove his point.

★ ★ ★

WHILE MAKING a routine inspection of Gene's Villa restaurant, 3315 12th Ave. S.W., about 2:20 p.m., he smelled what he thought was scorching wood. Wood smoke in a restaurant being against the principles he has been setting down for four years, he followed his nose to the source.

The source was in the kitchen where the owner's wife, Mrs. Gene Cioni, was cooking spaghetti. Officer Marks put his hand against the bottom of the wall behind the stove—Presto! —the top of the wall burst into flame.

He turned in an alarm and he and Mrs. Cioni fought the blaze with extinguishers and buckets of water.

By the time the Fire Department arrived, the fire was out and Officer Marks' class in fire prevention was finished for the day.

Gene's La Villa Supper Club

(ORIGINATOR OF CALGARY'S ITALIAN CUISINES)

a la Carte Menu

Minimum Service Charge $1.50 per person

Individual Anchovie Salad served with meals.

SOUPS

Chicken with Rice	.30
Vegetable Soup	.25
Lipton Noodle	.25
Pasta E Fagioli	.40
Minestrone	.40

APPETIZERS

French Fried Tomatoes	.75
French Fried Onions	.75
Anchovies (side order)	.50
Antipasto for 4	1.50
Celery Hearts	.35
Green Olives	.60
Pickled Herring (side order)	.50
Ripe Olives	.50
Salami (side order)	.75
Tomato Juice Cocktail	.25
Crab Meat Cocktail	.75
Shrimp Cocktail	.75
Vinegar Pickled Banana Peppers	.50
Assorted Antipasto on Request	

PASTI DISHES

Ravioli	1.50
Ravioli with Fried Chicken	1.75
Rigatoni with Mushrooms	1.75
Spaghetti with Fried Chicken	1.75
Spaghetti with Garlic or Hot Sauce	1.50
Spaghetti with Meat Sauce	1.50
Spaghetti with Meat Balls	1.50
Spaghetti Milanese	1.75
Spaghetti with Mushrooms	1.75
Spaghetti with Spareribs	1.75
Spaghetti with Italian Sausage	1.50
Spavioli	1.50
Spavioli with Meatballs	1.75
Spavioli with Chicken	2.00

GENE'S SPECIAL ITALIAN DINNER

Shrimp Cocktail	Crab Meat Cocktail
Soup	Salad
	Spavioli	
Half Fried Milkfed Spring Chicken	T-Bone Steak, Selected Red Brand Meat
DESSERT	**BEVERAGE**

$4.50

Cooked to your taste.

PIZZA PIE GIARDINIERE

Approx. 30 min. to prepare

1.50

Extra Romano Cheese	.25	Extra Sauce	.25

Each dish is freshly perpared as ordered. Please allow a few minutes.

Please respect the law. The consumption and/or possession of liquor on the premises is not permitted.

We are not responsible for lost articles.

GRILLED MEATS

Mexican Hot Tomales	1.50
Breaded Veal Cutlets with Bordelaise Sauce and French Fried	1.50
Chili Con Carne with Toast	1.50
Half Fried Milkfed Spring Chicken Cacciatore Style or Plain	
Veal Steak with Mushrooms	2.00
T-Bone Steak, Selected Red Brand Meat	2.50
Veal Scalopine with Green Peppers and Mushrooms	~~3.00~~ 300
Green Pepper Omelette	1.75
Grilled Italian Sausage with Green Peppers	1.50
Fried Mushrooms on Toast	1.75
Fried Shrimp	1.75
	1.75

DESSERTS

Pies, Various	.15
A la Mode	.20
Roquefort Cheese	.30
Strawberry Sundae	.25
Vanilla Ice Cream	.10

BEVERAGES

Bottled Soft Drinks, Small Large	.15
Coffee	.50
Milk	.10
Tea	.10
	.10

New business cards for "Gene's La Villa," January 1954.

Ten

THAT'S AMORE

LIKE ALL OTHER ASPECTS OF
CULTURE, TASTE IS A PRODUCT
OF HISTORY AND CHANGES
WITH TIME AND LOCATION.

—Alberto Capatti and Massimo
Montanari, *Italian Cuisine: A Cultural
History*

"I'D LIKE to try something different," said Barbara Bishop, closing the La Villa menu.

"I'm going to bring you something special," responded Gene. It had been eight years since my father had opened his first Italian restaurant, and being asked for suggestions was still music to his ears. Returning to the table with a small oval platter of chicken livers, he held the dish to her nose so she could take in the aroma, and then he set it down. Taking the two serving spoons into his right hand, he scooped a few small livers with golden onions and dark green peppers onto a side plate. "Take a small amount of the liver together with a bit of the vegetable," he counselled. Barbara glided the side of her fork through the pink interior of the liver and followed the cook's instructions. The combination of flavours and textures brought a wide smile and nod.

By the time La Villa opened in 1952, Gene's growing clientele had eaten their way through a menu that made them more knowledgeable about Italian food and more open in their tastes. My father assessed his former menu, item by item, to determine how he could improve the best-selling dishes and what new and unexpected foods he might add. Next to pasta, Gene's number one seller was steak. He had noticed that customers were leaving the delicious steak juices on their plates, so he added two slices of toasted Italian bread, brushed with a mixture of garlic, olive oil, and butter. Patrons used the garlic bread to sponge up the succulent juices.

When my father moved to La Villa, he had to find a good butcher nearby. His search ended when he found a dependable supply of premium beef at the Safeway store on 17th Avenue and 14th Street. He met with the head butcher and placed a standing order of fifty eight-ounce filet mignons, for small appetites, and fifty T-bones for the Saturday crowd alone, negotiating a price that, over the years, ranged from fifty-nine to sixty-nine cents per pound. Each T-bone had to be one inch thick for even cooking and by 1954, Gene was ordering one hundred sixteen-ounce steaks for Saturday night, offering a one-pound T-bone steak dinner for three dollars.

The popularity of breaded veal cutlets, pan-fried chicken, and chicken cacciatore never waned, but Gene knew that deep-fried foods were gaining in popularity in the United States, where Kentucky Fried Chicken was booming. He added golden crisp, deep-fried chicken to the menu, but it was never as popular as the Italian-style chicken he had created in 1950.

Onion rings were also gaining in popularity, but my father didn't have the patience to slice, dip, and deep-fry the individual rings. Hoping to deter customers' requests, he charged a premium for them, but the orders mounted. Then Nature intervened when a small field mouse got into the kitchen. Father chased after it with a broom, and the mouse panicked and tried to run across the bubbling oil in the deep fryer. "Son of a bitch!" cried Father. He shut off the equipment and drained and discarded the oil and the crispy rodent. The fryer was scoured and disinfected again and again, putting the machine out of commission for a week. Gene was still reluctant, but in 1954 he listed onion rings on his menu, à la carte, in response to customers' requests for them as an accompaniment to steak.

Both my father and my brother enjoyed bubbling hot soup. In the mid-1950s, the interest in space rocketed, and dehydrated foods associated with space travel became very popular. Ahead of the trend, Gene added Lipton's chicken noodle soup and Campbell's vegetable soup to the menu. At La Villa, commercial soups cost twenty-five cents a bowl while homemade soup was thirty to forty cents. Children, including me, preferred the packaged variety, but everyone else wanted Gene's soup.

In landlocked Calgary in 1952, shrimp cocktail was a luxury item. The Palliser Hotel and La Villa were among the few to offer it. Priced at seventy-five cents, it was expensive. My father paid five dollars for a five-pound block of two hundred frozen jumbo shrimps. The staff defrosted, steamed, and peeled the beauties, careful to leave the tail intact, while Gene concocted a secret tangy sauce of ketchup, horseradish, lemon juice, and black pepper. He instructed his assistants to take an elegant footed glass dish, put shredded lettuce in the bottom, then six plump shrimps, and drizzle three teaspoons of his cocktail sauce on top. My mother suggested that he hook an extra shrimp on the side of the dish, like a curled finger beckoning the diner. A wedge of lemon sat on the glass saucer, opposite a small cocktail fork. My father's shrimp cocktail was designed to make a statement.

While shrimp cocktails were popular, my father didn't sell enough of them to use all of the defrosted shrimps. Needing another shrimp dish, he again took his inspiration from Antrodoco, where, on special occasions such as Christmas Eve, villagers prepared fish as fritters. Gene dipped the cleaned shrimps into a simple batter of flour and water, creating a thin, brittle coating that accentuated the chewy richness of the seafood. A sprinkle of salt and a squirt of lemon finished the new menu item. Shrimp fritters or, as they were listed on the menu, deep-fried jumbo shrimps were an instant hit.

The now-famous anchovy salad came in a larger portion on an oval salad platter. The breadsticks, crunchy with a slight sweetness, were the perfect contrast to the vinaigrette. In 1948, my father had conceived the idea of serving breadsticks, a specialty of Turin. He concluded they would be perfect for his restaurant—they didn't need slicing, they weren't filling, they didn't go stale, and the crunchy fingers could simply be stacked inside a cup on the table.

Since nothing like breadsticks existed in Calgary, my father had to find a bakery that could make them. So he took his idea to Martin's Bakery, kitty-corner from the Cecil Hotel. The kosher-only bakery had a reputation for quality. Mr. Martin was busy making bagels, but my father's idea caught his attention. "I have something new that I'd like you to make." My father explained that a breadstick was about six inches long and as round as a thumb. It was dry and crunchy. "Do you think you could make it?"

"Come back tomorrow. I'll have your breadsticks."

The next day, full of anticipation, my father entered the bakery, sniffing the yeasty sweetness. "I'll get them," said the owner and he brought out a pan. The size was right, but as soon as my father touched one, he knew the texture was wrong—sure enough, it was a long bagel. "I'll try again," said the baker.

The second time around, the pieces were firmer but still too soft in the centre. "I'm sorry, they won't do. They have to be hard enough to scoop up butter." My father resigned himself to serving rolls like everyone else, but the idea lingered in his mind for four more years. He tried again in 1952 with City Bakery, which was able to produce the proper breadstick. The waitresses stuffed eight into a coffee cup and placed it on the table with a small dish of salted butter. Customers put a pad of butter on their side plates and dipped the breadsticks before each bite. Not only were the treats gobbled up during dinner, patrons started taking them home. The bakery couldn't keep up with the demand.

One evening in 1953, when Leon Libin, owner of the Palace Bakery, was enjoying dinner at La Villa, my father told him about his breadstick supply problem. Leon assured my father that the large Palace Bakery could make them in quantity. My father provided the recipe, but didn't think to make it an exclusive arrangement. Breadsticks were soon available throughout the city, but customers still prized the La Villa ones to take home.

Another of Gene's culinary innovations was heralded by Dean Martin, singing from the jukebox: "When the moon hits your eye like a big pizza pie, that's amore."

"Hey, Gene," said an American customer, "I had a pizza pie in San Francisco and it was delicious. Can you make me one?"

"Sure, I know pizza. In Antrodoco, we put some vegetables and a little cheese on dough. We call it *pizza povera*, poor pizza, because we use whatever we have."

"Will you make it? I want pizza pie with everything on it."

"Give me a week," said Gene, and he started planning. Pizza took my father back nearly thirty years to Naples, where he had eaten the local specialty before boarding the ship for America. Closing his eyes, he could still remember the taste of the thin, crunchy crust and the sweetness of tomato with fruity olive oil.

My father determined that his pizza would be as memorable. He flattened the yeast dough with his floured hand, rolled it out a little more, and picked up an edge to stretch it. He flipped it in a circular motion with a twist of his wrist until the thin crust fit the new fourteen-inch pan. Lightly brushing some olive oil on the pan and across the dough, my father dealt pieces of mushrooms, green pepper, black olives, thin slices of salami, and tomatoes around the top. Then he scattered a few pieces of anchovy, spread dollops of sauce, and sprinkled grated mozzarella cheese sparingly. As with all his cooking, my father practised restraint and balance to keep the ingredients from overwhelming the crust. It was baked golden brown.

Gene proudly presented the pizza, cut into four pieces. As the customer chewed, he started shaking his head and smacking his lips. "Wonderful! I'm coming every week."

Word of the pizza got around quickly, and more and more people asked for it. Although my father had revelled in creating the first pizza in Calgary, he quickly grew bored with rolling out crust after crust. "I don't like making pizza every day!" he complained to my mother. "It takes too much time." She gave him a hug and then laughed at his solution. "I'm going to double the price to three dollars. Then people won't order it." His idea backfired—demand only grew faster. In 1953, my father capitulated and added pizza pie giardiniere, vegetable garden pizza, to the menu, reducing the price to $1.50 but warning that it took thirty minutes to prepare. It became one of the most popular items at Gene's La Villa.

Dr. Gelfand's new bride, Phyllis, chose pizza as her first meal at La Villa. She knew that her husband and Gene were good friends but she didn't know that Fortuna had been working overtime to bring my father to Dr. Sid Gelfand in 1948. Over the years "Doc" had treated my father's pneumonia, my burns, and minor family ailments. He was one of my father's first customers in the first restaurant. When my father found out that Gelfand was a bachelor recently moved from Canmore, he declared, "My spaghetti parlour is your home." The irony is that Doc didn't really like spaghetti, but he loved Gene's chicken, steak, veal, and anchovy salad. He also liked my father's enthusiasm, creativeness, and warmth, while my father admired Doc's intelligence and kindness. They were both very emotional men, short, bald, and soft-spoken, although Dr. Gelfand's voice had a distinctive rasp and my father's grew loud from excitement. It was fitting that Gene's first customer at La Villa was his friend and fan, Sid Gelfand.

Whenever Doc came in, my father fussed over him, and so when he brought his bride into La Villa in 1954, my father was overjoyed for his friend. Phyllis Gelfand immediately endeared herself to Gene when she asked him, "What do you recommend?" She enjoyed her choice of the pizza so much that she asked Gene for a simple recipe that she could make at home with ingredients that she might have on hand.

My father was caught off guard—customers didn't usually ask for his recipes. But, wanting to please Phyllis, he suggested a Calgary-style pizza that she could make at home. "It'll taste different, but still good. Try using a pie crust, no sugar though. Roll it very thin and mould it to the pan. Then sprinkle a little ground beef and onions that you've already browned, a little ketchup and some cheese. Mozzarella is perfect, but cheddar will do, but not too much."

It was not La Villa pizza, with Gene's balanced ingredients and thin crust, but it was a recipe, a little gift that he could give to his good friend's wife.

Besides pizza pie, some American customers asked for foods they had enjoyed at home, especially the southern states. They didn't distinguish between the various regional cuisines. To them, my father cooked "international" food; if he served Italian dishes, then why not Mexican hot tamales and chili con carne?

My father was surprised at first. In Italy, each region had its specialties and you wouldn't expect to have Bolognese meat sauce in Venice, where the specialty is fish. But he respected his customers' preferences and put the items on the menu. When an order came in, he opened a can of chili con carne and heated and served it, but he still shook his head a little.

My father never used a recipe or a measuring spoon—everything was prepared by taste and by feel. He found that cooking larger quantities, such as forty-six quarts of spaghetti sauce, was more complicated than merely multiplying the amount of ingredients. The intense flavour of the sauce decreased as the quantity increased. He fiddled, adding more herbs and trying different proportions of ingredients, but he was never quite satisfied with the taste.

Enjoying dinner at Linda Mae's Chinese restaurant one Monday evening, it suddenly hit my father that the soup and other dishes had very intense flavours and yet the cook must be preparing large batches just like he did. He was off to the kitchen, returning with the answer, a robin's egg–blue tin. "Marta, the cook uses this in everything."

"Is it an age-old Chinese secret?" snickered Gary.

"Not any more." Mother grinned.

The next day Gene added a tablespoon of the Chinese powder to the spaghetti sauce. Waiting, smelling, and finally sipping, his taste buds warmed and then exploded. "This is it, Marta. The flavour's perfect!" he cried. My father continued to experiment and found that a teaspoon sprinkled into the meatball mixture, another into the vinaigrette, and a tablespoon into the chicken soup returned the intense flavours.

From that time on, every few months my father drove across town to Chinatown, on Centre Street, to purchase another blue tin. He climbed up three flights of narrow stairs to a battered wooden door. Inside were lopsided towers of ceramic dishes and cooking pans, barrels of soup ladles, drawers of cleavers of all sizes, assorted packages of unknown delicacies stacked on shelves, and a section of dry herbs and roots in bottles crammed in wooden cubbyholes in the back wall. Earthen crocks of duck eggs and another crock with the stench of hundred-year-old garlic stewed beside the counter. My father pointed to the light blue tin, watching as the frail clerk hung like a spider to reach the prize. Gene was too absorbed to notice the stares and little over-the-shoulder glances from other patrons. On one visit, my father bought a large Chinese meat cleaver that he thought perfect for hacking through pork spareribs. "Look!" he showed my mother, "I bet I'm the only Italian in Calgary with a Chinese cleaver."

My father was fanatical about using quality ingredients. With the instincts of an explorer, he passionately foraged for new foods and dependable suppliers. The first challenge had been sourcing quality dried spaghetti. Italians had high regard for good dried "macaroni," as they called all dried noodles, some even preferring its thinner strands to the broader homemade ones. In Riverside, it was a luxury to buy macaroni, so for a rare treat, in the early days, Gisetta ordered Unico spaghetti and rigatoni at the neighbourhood store. Unico was the most expensive brand because the company was located in Toronto and their products had to be shipped by rail to Calgary, but Gene and Gisetta believed they were worth it. She and my father agreed that Unico spaghetti tasted very much like "the macaroni made in the little Antrodoco factory." The choice for La Villa was obvious; Gene served Unico, just as he had in his other restaurants.

Unico's partner, Toronto Macaroni, made the spaghetti using hard durum semolina wheat, similar to the fine pasta my father remembered. In the fall of 1949, Catelli Foods of Montreal built a large macaroni factory in Lethbridge, one hundred miles south of Calgary. The plant manager dropped off a case of spaghetti at the Dine and Dance. "Here, Gene, it's free. I can guarantee same-day delivery on your order. Send it by truck, no high rail freight charges."

"Thanks. I wish you luck, but I use Unico."

"Just try it, that's all I ask."

"Okay, but no promises."

Gene cooked the spaghetti but never served it; he couldn't accept its sticky texture. Catelli management tried for years to change my father's mind, even inviting him to tour the factory.

Finally, returning from Easter vacation in Great Falls, Montana, in 1953, we stopped in Lethbridge for a private tour. I remember tall vats and workers dressed in white. Gary told me, "If you aren't good, we'll leave you here to work. You'll be in spaghetti heaven."

Wanting to support local farmers and industry, my father unlocked the trunk of the Hudson and watched the complimentary cases being loaded. The next day, he opened the twenty-pound box and boiled a handful; the cooked product was just as before. Gene was loyal to Unico products all through his business years because they met his high standard.

By the time La Villa was in full swing, my father had a standing monthly order at Unico for fifty twenty-pound cases of spaghetti, fifteen cases of rigatoni, and ten of linguine. Each case cost six dollars. My father added rigatoni to the menu in 1954 to provide another taste and texture. He liked the shape of the noodles because the tubes were easy to eat and captured more sauce. For the opposite reason he chose linguine to complement the delicate veal dishes because it didn't hold much sauce. He put both Romano and Parmesan cheeses, imported from Parma, on his list. The Romano came as a large wheel with a logo stamped on the outside rind, and the log of Parmesan arrived huddled in a wooden crate. The cheese cost two dollars per pound. Gene insisted on using Gallo olive oil imported from Italy. At six dollars for a three-litre tin, it was the costliest item, but my father believed it was well worth the expense. Canadians used vegetable oil—it was the unfamiliar mellow, fruity olive oil that underpinned the unique taste of his cooking. Finally, he ordered a few dozen cases holding six one hundred-ounce cans each of his beloved Abruzzese Italian plum tomatoes, each case costing eight dollars.

"Come on, Gary, we have to get the Unico order from Toronto," called Father one day. It was a forty-minute drive to the train station downtown, but Gene sped there in thirty minutes. "Start loading and I'll go pay," he told Gary.

Gene the businessman zeroed in on the shipping charge as he fingered the wad of bills in his pocket. As a westerner, he thought the freight was exorbitant, and he was incensed each year when the rates increased. "What the hell!" he'd say. "The distance doesn't change." Rumours were rampant that the Canadian Board of Transport Commissioners was considering an increase of nearly nine per cent in 1954, making it cheaper to buy California tomato juice than Canadian. My father was livid that it cost more to ship from Toronto to Calgary than it did to ship from Toronto to Vancouver. "Damn it! The train has to go right past Calgary to go to Vancouver." Adding to the insult, it was cheaper to send freight from the west to Toronto.

Father paid several hundred dollars to the agent and returned to help Gary. With the trunk and the back seat laden with hundreds of pounds of Italian bounty, my father was forced to drive his sagging car home slowly. "I hate this trip. It takes so long. We fly here and have to crawl back. When you're sixteen, I'm buying you a car," Father told Gary. "And you can do this on your own."

It took nearly an hour to unload and store the boxes at La Villa. As always, Gary carried one of the cases of spaghetti into the kitchen. Taking a large knife, Father split the brown paper tape running the length of the cardboard box and pressed the flaps back to reveal the inky purple-blue paper protecting the macaroni. Carefully, he folded back the heavy paper and scooped out a handful to cook for dinner. The ceremony of cooking spaghetti from a newly opened box made it an extra treat.

In addition to cooking commercial pasta, my father made fresh ravioli three times a week. He served five squares fanned in a circle and large enough to share, but ravioli fanatics preferred the main course of ten, covering an entire plate. In fact, customer indecision inspired my father to create a new word, spavioli, for a dinner offering of a half order each of ravioli and spaghetti.

Gene made his ravioli extra large to minimize preparation time; he folded a tablespoon of meat in feather-light dough, forming a three-inch square. Sometimes I helped my father make them, standing on a chair to reach the counter. "Take the fork like this and stab," he instructed,

Gene's Lasagna

(Serves 6)

My father learned Gisetta's secret for making the perfect consistency of dough—start with the eggs and add a half eggshell of water per egg. The quantity of flour required is dictated by the egg-water mixture. The ingredients will be determined by the size of pan and amount of lasagna to be made.

Meat mixture:

1 lb. each ground beef or veal, and pork

1 lb. sliced mushrooms

1 tsp. each oregano, basil, salt, and pepper

Dough:

3 eggs

3 half eggshells of water

½ tsp. salt

Flour

3 cups spaghetti sauce

Romano and/or Parmesan cheese, grated

Sauté meat and add remaining ingredients for the meat mixture. Set aside. Mix eggs, water, and salt. Gradually add flour, mixing until the dough no longer sticks to hands. Let rest for 20 minutes, then cut pieces and put through pasta roller several times, finishing with the roller on the second- or third-finest setting. Boil lasagna noodles in salted water until they float to the top. Remove and put in a pan of cold water and pat dry. Noodles are ready for assembly with the meat mixture.

To assemble: Put enough spaghetti sauce to cover the bottom of an oblong pan. Alternate the noodles, meat mixture, a light dusting of grated Romano/Parmesan cheese, and spaghetti sauce. (Be careful not to put in too much sauce.) End with a noodle layer on top, add sauce and cheese.

Cover with foil and bake at 325°F for 60 minutes, depending on pan size. Remove foil, cook an additional 15 minutes, so that the top crisps, just the way Gary liked it.

putting his hand over mine to demonstrate how to prick the top of the little mounds. "This is a very important job. If it isn't done right, the ravioli will explode when I cook them." The word "explode" sounded so outrageous in our little ravioli world that we both laughed. By the age of five, I had advanced to the art of pressing the fork tines around the ravioli edges to seal in the filling. But to me, it was all playtime with Daddy, and after a while I was off to find the cats.

My father prepared homemade lasagna and gnocchi from scratch, for special occasions. It took time and skill. His lasagna was derived from the legacy that the Romans had bequeathed to Antrodoco, with tomato sauce only, no balsamella. He felt that the heavier white sauce overwhelmed the lasagna noodles, whereas his tomato sauce, sparingly used, sweetened it. Gene's lasagna consisted of about eight layers of ultra-thin noodles, spread with sautéed ground veal and pork with herbs, modest amounts of tomato sauce, and grated Romano and Parmesan cheeses, sprinkled judiciously. The finished lasagna was covered with foil and refrigerated until needed. He baked it for an hour covered and another fifteen minutes uncovered to ensure that the top noodles were crisp, especially in the corners, which he saved as a treat for Gary.

Gnocchi, likely the first pasta that the Romans made, was equally labour-intensive. My father produced light little pillows of potato pasta. Occasionally, when overwhelmed with orders, he hired women from Antrodoco to assist him, but mostly he prepared these specialties in the afternoons, when he might otherwise retreat upstairs for a nap. Gisetta had taught him the recipe and technique twenty-five years before, but now, with the small pieces of dough strewn across his La Villa kitchen, my father called me, his five-year-old daughter from the loading dock. "Maria, it's gnocchi time."

"Take a piece," my father instructed. "Now, with this finger—he tapped the pointer finger—roll the dough over the back of the fork tines like this." I picked up the technique nearly as quickly as he had. "What you're doing is very important. Those ridges you're making will hold more tomato sauce." For gnocchi time, my father always chose my favourite song, Julius La Rosa singing "Eh Cumpari." This crazy song had us singing, dancing, and rolling until we had covered all the surfaces in the kitchen with hundreds of little white lumps. My father placed them on trays lined with waxed paper, put them in the refrigerator, and said, "Thanks for your help, Maria. I'll cook some for your dinner."

Finding good-quality vegetables posed one of the greatest challenges. Calgary's short growing season meant using imported vegetables for most of the year, and it was difficult to find reasonable prices and adequate supplies. In fact, the quality and availability of vegetables dictated which dishes my father offered. He always had soup on the menu because abundant root vegetables could be used. My father's decision to offer french fries was not based on requests, but on the availability of the ubiquitous spud. Mushrooms grew in darkness on local farms and were readily available. Gene used imported dried herbs extensively and narrowed the fresh produce down to root vegetables, onions, celery, garlic, green peppers, lemons, and parsley.

Father trolled the stalls of the City Hall Market and the aisles of Safeway, going into small neighbourhood stores to find the best produce. He luxuriated in the seasonal bounty. He first found the Tamagi family stall in the City Hall Market in the mid-1940s, buying their fine Lethbridge produce—lettuce, celery, green peppers—for the Burns Meat Packing cafeteria. As Gene started his first Italian restaurant, the Tamagis opened Bridge Brand Produce Company, with a warehouse in town to store produce from the Okanagan

LA VILLA SUPPER CLUB

New Year's Eve

Jamboree

Dancing — Novelties — Turkey Dinner

$4.50 per Person   N.° 300

Valley and California. Bridge Brand and Horne and Pitfield Foods were the wholesalers from whom my father bought quality vegetables throughout the 1950s.

A lot of pop was sold at La Villa and my father made a nice profit charging fifteen cents for a bottle that cost him six cents to buy. He knew that his customers were either the Coca-Cola crowd who drank rum or the 7-Up group preferring a "7 and 7," Seagram's Seven Blended Whisky and 7-Up. Most kids drank pop straight, with a straw, as the perfect accompaniment to spaghetti and meatballs, although my mother always handed me a glass of milk, telling me that pop would "rot my teeth."

Each week, a large truck from Polar Aerated Water Works pulled up to the loading dock. As a child, I thought it odd that the truck had shelves along the sides. The driver popped out, put on gloves, and began to pull off a dozen wooden crates and stack them on the dock. The twenty-four seven-ounce glass bottles of 7-Up and Crush tinkled as they tapped one another. Orange Crush bottles were stubby brown beauties with ridges that fit nicely in a little hand. I preferred them to the slim green bottles of 7-Up, but then Orange Crush was my favourite kind of pop. My father carried a few cases into the restaurant and then Gary or one of the waitresses loaded them into the cooler.

Five years after my father had opened Gene's Spaghetti Parlor with its chalkboard menu of three items, the cook had expanded La Villa's menu to a couple of dozen main courses. Some of them—pizza, fried shrimps, and veal scaloppine—were introduced for the first time in Calgary. More important than the number of choices was the fact that my father had passed on his love of well-prepared food to his customers. Every Saturday night at La Villa was a well-planned feast; the guests had become friends; my father's creativity had resulted in crowds of customers. Perhaps Barbara Bishop said it best with her toast, "To Gene, our friend and the best cook in the Calgary, for guiding us to new taste experiences."

|Eleven|

PIONEER CELEBRITY CHEF AND THE RESTAURANT SUBCULTURE

ANTRODOCO WAS FAMOUS
FOR FOOD, [BUT] GENE
WAS THE ONLY PERSON
COMING OUT OF ANTRODOCO
TO COMMERCIALIZE IT.

—Dante Poscente

"HELLO, Martha, it's Harry from the Palliser. Four of us will be at La Villa in an hour. Tell Gene we're starving. Mario says he wants the usual."

The message was relayed to the kitchen. "Okay," said my father. "I'll set aside the remaining steaks. Tell me when they're here."

My mother returned to the dining room to scan for a table. "Stella, check the party beside the fireplace. See if you can move them along." By the time the Palliser gang arrived, a newly set table awaited.

Mario Grassi went to the kitchen. "*Come sta?*" he greeted Gene.

"*Sto bene.* Good! I'm good," Gene said, putting his arm around the elegant man's shoulder. "So you want the usual. How is it to be back at the Palliser? We'll talk when I bring your food."

Mario had brought a bottle of Chianti, knowing that it was the only wine Gene would drink, apart from some homemade brew. He pulled out a chair, poured the cook a glass, and watched his *paesano* add water to cut the wine's rawness. The Palliser gang raised their glasses, and Mario toasted, "To the one and only Gene and his food. *Salute.*"

By the summer of 1949, my father had become a celebrity chef. Just six months after opening his first restaurant, he'd made a name for himself, and his reputation grew with each new restaurant. "Let's go to Gene's" said it all. Entertainers performing in town came to Gene's for a late supper. Louis Armstrong, Sarah Vaughan, Duke Ellington, Count Basie, Lionel Hampton, and Billie Ekstein all said the food was excellent. These entertainers, sports figures, and business people told friends

The final renovation at La Villa, September 1952.

Gene's Dine and Dance, 1950. Standing, left to right: Ivo Brandelli, Adelmo Brandelli. Seated, left to right: Mario Grassi, Julie Grassi, Mario Brandelli.

in New York, Los Angeles, Las Vegas, and Seattle about Gene, and customers from these places came to Calgary to seek him out. In a time before restaurant critics, it was Gene's patrons who gave him the best reviews.

When the Fabulous Fifties began, my father was already enjoying success in Gene's Spaghetti Dine and Dance. Calgary's economy was on fire and many people were interested in opening new restaurants. Some of Gene's friends were caught up in the frenzy. When he heard that Ivo and Aurora Brandelli and Dante Signori were planning to open an Italian restaurant, my father counselled them to be modest in their plans, giving freely of the lessons he had learned. They opened the Venetian Gardens Restaurant in July 1950 in downtown Calgary. To my father's surprise, Mario and his wife, Julie, bought in as well.

Gene went to visit the place. Billed as "Calgary's Most Characteristic Restaurant," it was ornately decorated and there was live music and entertainment nightly. It took only one look for my father to know that the restaurant was a high economic risk. He cautioned Mario that too much money had gone into the decor, money that would be better spent on the food, and warned that the rent and taxes would swallow the profits.

It was too late; the Grassis had made their decision. Julie, a good cook, was in the kitchen, but restaurant preparation was difficult. It required timing, organization of others, and knowledge of customer preferences, which came only from experience. Mario ran the dining room with the tact and decorum he had perfected during his thirty-five years at the Palliser Hotel, but there were few customers during the week. Once executives and workers had left their downtown offices to go home, they had no desire to return to the centre of town for dinner. The brutality of the restaurant business smashed the dreams of the Venetian Gardens' owners, and it closed after little more than a year.

"What will you do now?" my father asked a weary Mario. Having been at the Palliser for most of his working life, rising to assistant captain of the dining room, Mario negotiated a return to the hotel.

During the fifties, only one other Italian restaurant opened, or rather, reopened. Louis Carloni redecorated what had been my father's second restaurant and in March 1954 launched it as the Isle of Capri, but it was never competition for Gene's La Villa.

There was, however, one restaurant that my father saw as competition from the day its doors opened in September 1951. This was the Pump Room, in the basement of the new high-rise Petroleum Building. Executives of the Petroleum Building had sunk more than $100,000 into the interior of the luxurious restaurant. My father had to see it for himself, so he called the manager for a tour.

Even Gene was impressed by the grandeur of the huge dining room, with its sweeping moon-shaped, copper art deco ceiling. His gaze settled on a table covered with crisp cream linen and matching napkins and upon which sat grey and maroon dishes bordered by heavy silverware, the same silverware used in the House of Commons. "How about this menu?" asked the manager, proudly displaying a sheet of creamy parchment. "Every day the new items are written in copper ink."

My father whistled softly. "How many staff?"

"Thirty" buzzed in his ears. It was five times Gene's payroll—that is, the weekend payroll, when an extra teenager helped to serve. Competing with the opulence and resources of the Pump Room was impossible, but my father knew his food was equal, if not better.

La Villa business was so good that my parents renovated again in August 1952, adding a gas furnace and a dance floor with side alcoves for larger parties. After settling the details with Nick Corradetti, my father excitedly started planning our summer holiday route. We would visit restaurants and nightclubs in Montana and Idaho to seek out the latest trends. My father constantly gathered information about restaurants in San Francisco, Chicago, and New York. In America, the land of the cocktail, there was always something to learn.

One beautiful Monday morning, we set off in the Hudson Wasp. By then, I was a pro at falling asleep instantly to avoid car sickness. Several hours later, the sound of laughter woke me. I heard Gary reciting, "Cattle crossing means go slow. That old bull is some cow's beau … Burma-Shave."

Then my mother spoke. "This one's for you, Gene. Around the curve lickety-split. Beautiful car Wasn't it? … Burma-Shave."

It was a year before I understood that they were reading the Burma-Shave advertisements that lined the highway.

Like many Calgarians, we travelled to Great Falls, Montana, because the prices were cheaper (thanks to a higher Canadian dollar), the quality was good, and the styles were avant-garde. While we shopped, my father went to visit his friend Eddie Newman.

Depending on the time of day, Eddie was either at Gus and Eddie's Lounge or his restaurant, the Deluxe Steak House Lounge. Eddie told my father, "Customers want live entertainment. They'll come out, have a drink, and maybe some dinner and watch a show or even listen to an organist."

"I guess serving alcohol is way more profitable than food," admitted my father.

"You bet! We're turning the steak house into a nightclub with a new name, the 3Ds. That's for drinking, dining, and dancing."

"You know, Eddie, at La Villa, my cooking is the entertainment. Sure, I want my customers to enjoy a drink with their food. Eating's about good food, good friends, and a drink. But focusing on drink— that's not me. I'm about food. Food is why my customers socialize, why I socialize. That's what makes La Villa!"

"Well, Gene, you think that way because you're a cook! Me, I'm a businessman. I go where the money is."

My father shook Eddie's hand. "Good luck. I've got to pick the family up at the Bon Marché store."

"Next time you're in town, bring them by for dinner and see the floor show." Eddie waved and watched the Wasp peel down the street.

We were off to Idaho, stopping for cheeseburgers and fries in

Sandpoint at Dusty Miller's diner. My father went into the kitchen and said, "I want to know everything about your french fries, starting with the kind of potatoes you use." Dusty's french fries were crispy and non-greasy, and they tasted like a real potato, which is why my father wanted to reproduce them to accompany his steaks. Like Dusty's, my father's french fries were made from potatoes peeled daily and cooked to order.

Coeur d'Alene was the next stop. We had dinner at Templin's Grill, a beautiful restaurant on the lakeshore. Robert Templin, the owner, came by like Gene always did at La Villa to ask if we were enjoying dinner. "Yes," replied Gene, "and I like the view of the water. It's peaceful. I have a restaurant, too. Let me introduce myself."

"I'm planning to build an adjacent motel to take advantage of the scenery. It'll draw travellers to the restaurant, too," confided Templin.

"You know, Bob, my La Villa's opposite a golf course and I've got a few acres around the restaurant. I think it would be a perfect place for a hotel some day."

On that trip my father noticed that restaurants were beginning to focus on a particular niche, and it gave him some satisfaction that he had anticipated this trend. Gene specialized in Italian food in 1949, and new restaurants with other specialties followed. The newer Chinese

Gary, Father, and me in front of the Hudson car in Great Falls, Montana, April 1953.

restaurants—the Purple Lantern and Linda Mae's—bore little resemblance to the Chinese-owned cafés that had come when the railway was built. They now described menu items in English, and patrons sat at tables with linen tablecloths, served by staff ready to give advice. The Town and Country introduced Calgary to the buffet, and in October 1954 the Starlight Room in the Royal Hotel offered a more exotic version, the "smorgasbord," on Wednesday evenings from 6:00 to 10:00 PM. In 1955, a contractor named Ed Jaeger built a new housing subdivision about a mile west of La Villa and a restaurant called the Lone Pine Supper Club. It was a high-end place, a precursor of the nightclub, offering a sweeping view of the city. Beautiful cigarette girls in seductive black strapless costumes roamed among the guests. The Lone Pine offered steaks and dancing to live music, but it was "too much about show" for my father's taste.

Calgarians loved steak, as my father well knew, and Gene's friend Hy Aisenstat had a great idea. "Hy's opening a steak house downtown," he reported to my mother. "Hy figures he'll attract the business crowd and tourists." My mother continued writing a cheque to the Calgary Natural Gas Company, the January 1956 invoice in front of her, and she didn't look up. "He's going to build a big grill in the middle of the dining room and surround it with glass. Customers can watch the cooks. I've always sworn by an open kitchen but now … now, it's a cook under glass!" Father's laughter rippled down his body, forcing him to double over.

Mother finally looked up. "I hope that his wife realizes how hard it is to raise a family AND start a new business. Maybe we should talk to them."

The Aisenstats opened Hy's Steak House in a second-floor loft at a cost of about $30,000. Like my parents, they had a good idea at the right time, concentrating on food cooked right before your eyes. Eventually they created a chain of successful steak houses across Canada.

Meanwhile, there were businessmen more interested in liquor sales than in food. They found a loophole in the stringent Alberta liquor laws: private clubs were allowed to sell alcohol to their members. The Al San Club and the Harris Club Sky Rooms were private clubs. Their members bought drinks, but they had to sign chits listing the kinds of drink and the names of the drinkers. In December 1955, Cliff Harris targeted women, establishing "the first and only Ladies' cocktail club in Calgary."

Yearly, we went to Great Falls and visited Eddie Newman, enjoying dinner at his 3DS nightclub. My father saw that many of Eddie's customers didn't eat; they drank and watched the floor show, and they didn't mind paying high prices. Now Gene was curious to see what was happening in other parts of the United States. In 1956 we drove to Seattle, because he had heard good things about Italian restaurants there. We went to Rosellini's, where he introduced himself to Victor Rosellini, the owner. We ate delicious spaghetti with shrimps and drank red wine—even I got some. Gene told Victor his favourite joke about an Italian father who comes home to find his young son sneaking a cup of coffee. "What's the matter with you?" shouts the outraged father. "Throw that out, and drink your wine!"

Victor's mother was also an accomplished cook and restaurateur, and the next night, with Victor, we ate at her Roma Cafe. Platters of spaghetti and rigatoni came and then plates of fresh grilled fish. While Mother, Gary, and I enjoyed our cassata ice cream, the three chefs discussed the liquor laws. "The liquor laws changed here in '49, and we could serve a drink with dinner," said Mama Rosellini. "People lost interest in the private clubs. Instead they came to the restaurants to enjoy good food with their cocktails and wine."

"That's when a lot of good restaurants sprang up here," acknowledged Victor.

"The same will happen in Alberta," my father predicted, "and I'm going to help it happen soon."

They lifted their glasses. "To change and to success for our families," my father said in Italian.

Gene wanted his customers to be able to relax—no more hiding a bottle under the table or waiting for the police to finish their rounds. More Calgarians were travelling south and experiencing the unfettered joys of the three D's. Why not in Calgary?

Meanwhile, American tourists were perplexed and annoyed that they couldn't enjoy a cocktail with dinner in Calgary. Local restaurateurs were seething over lost opportunities to make money. "Alberta is second to none—our liquor laws stink!" slammed the president of the Canadian Restaurant Association at its Calgary convention in 1955. Tourists were going to British Columbia instead, where new liquor laws had approved cocktail lounges and drinking with dinner.

"What are you guys doing?" Gene asked his friend Fred Colborne, the local Member of the Legislative Assembly in fall 1957. "You've been at La Villa on the weekend. You've seen customers enjoy a drink with dinner. Do they get drunk? No! Drinking's part of socializing. Would I stand for drunk customers? No! It would ruin my business. Fred, please tell the premier not to stop change. It's bad for everyone if he does."

A few months later, Gene read that the new Liquor Act would be introduced for first reading on 28 March 1958 by Fred Colborne, minister without portfolio, and he was pleased that his conversation might have hastened the change. He wished that he could have been as successful with the city planners, who, by rejecting his application to build a new La Villa, had derailed his plans for an elegant venue that would serve fine wines and alcohol with dinner.

As soon as the new law was proclaimed in the fall of 1958, two Calgary restaurants and six hotels applied to serve liquor in dining lounges and cocktail bars: the Pump Room; Ging's Supper Lounge; the Palliser, Wales, Royal, York, and Crossroads hotels; and Barney's Fine Foods in the Stampeder Hotel. In late November 1958, when the new businesses opened, they were swamped. Droves of diners were turned away at lunch and dinner.

It was a very good sign for the next wave of applicants: the newly rebuilt Lone Pine Supper Club, the Skyline Restaurant, and the Beacon Hotel. The Beacon Hotel featured the Caribbean Room, specializing in seafood, with a large lobster tank as an attraction, and the Calypso Lounge, with waiters in Hawaiian shirts with puffed sleeves, recreating the South Seas in an American fashion. The success of this group of restaurants, in turn, prompted Eamon's Restaurant, the Nag-Wey (co-owned by my father's friend, police sergeant Percy Weyman), Child's Restaurant, and the Airways (the airport restaurant) to enter the next round of licensing. Just as the three chefs had discussed in Seattle, the legalization of drinking ushered in the modern era of dining in Calgary.

|Twelve|

Please join Gene and Martha Cioni for a private party
in appreciation of the support of their patrons
At Gene's La Villa Restaurant
Monday, April 17, 1954, 8:00 p.m.

꧁ **A NUDGE** ꧂
OF TIME

I WAS AWARE
OF REAL TIME PASSING
AS ONE IS AWARE OF
THE FLOWING OF A REAL
STREAM, THAT IS,
IN A CONTINUALLY
VARYING WAY …

—Ignazio Silone,
The Seed Beneath the Snow,
in *The Abruzzo Trilogy*

"WE'LL send out maybe a hundred invitations and probably sixty will come," suggested my father.

"That'll be a nice-sized crowd," agreed my mother. "I'll make a list."

They sent invitations to my father's family: Auntie Gisetta (even though my father didn't think she'd come) and my cousins Connie, Nino, the Amanteas, and Nick and Stella Corradetti. My father asked Reno Corradetti, now an established photographer, to take pictures. My mother's family was few on these occasions since Sam and Goldie Ross had moved to Toronto—just Uncle Manuel and Aunt Annie. They invited several Calgary Gun Club members: Vera Holdsworth and her mother, Mary Harris; the Hansons; Mikkelsons; and McLennans. Since my father loved the Hudson he'd purchased from Hammill Motors, he invited the Hammills. Then he invited all fourteen members of the Rowe party and the Palliser gang: Grassis, Aloros, Johnny Luvisotto, Harry Heath, Jean Craig, Kay Prozak, and Archie Mackinnon were asked. They added the Belzbergs, Singers, Libins, Pearlmans, Kalefs, Cohens, and Gelfands. There were invitations to politicians: McIntoshes, Colbournes, Art Smith, and Harold Riley; to police friends, the Gouldies and Weymans; and to Dave

Gene and Martha's annual party for their patrons, April 1955.
(Photo by Ted Fitch)

Reynolds and Norm Bruce, city food inspectors. They invited Catholics and Italians: the LoVecchios and Mary Comella; Florence Thorpe; Father Tim; the Brandellis; and Julio Poscente, Sofia's son, and his wife, Maureen. Bill Morrow's company put my father's favourite Italian songs on the Wurlitzer, so the Morrows were included. Football fans Hazel Dixon and Rolly Bradley and Harry Young were on the list—and Sugarfoot Anderson, of course.

On Saturday, the Rowe party sent a spectacular bouquet of fragrant spring flowers. The group saw the colourful display between two tall candlesticks atop the fireplace as they entered La Villa. "Thank you for the flowers," my father said, hugging the ladies. "But you know, in Italy, we only send flowers for funerals."

My parents stood at the entrance to the dining room, receiving the stream of guests. My father hugged everyone, including the men, but my mother kissed only those whom she knew well. They were relaxed and laughing, enjoying each other just as much as they enjoyed their friends.

"It's odd to see the two of you together," Vivian Rowe remarked. "You're such a handsome couple!"

"I agree," said Mary Harris, "and a wonderful team."

"We might even dance tonight!" my father blurted, kissing his Marta's hand.

"Make yourselves at home. Sit where you like. It's an Italian-style party tonight," commented Mother.

Guests quickly filled the dining room and introduced themselves to one another; then they filled the dance floor. Gene had set up a small bar in the corner of the foyer and joked with friends waiting for a refill. "No police tonight?" asked one.

"Only a few enjoying the party," laughed my father, winking at Stan Gouldie and Percy Weyman.

Father Tim was table hopping. "I don't dance, but I get around," he told my cousin Connie. She laughed. "When I saw you at the St. Francis Retreat House, you were so serious."

"Well, that was work and this is … fun."

Reno Corradetti corralled people for a photo with the hosts. "Later, I'll get a group pose," he said.

"Sure, roam around. Get some good shots," my father told his stepbrother.

My father had set up long communal tables, the way they did for celebrations in Antrodoco. He and his staff had set out trays of Italian cold meats, cheeses, and breadsticks on the tables for guests to sample at their leisure.

"Where are Gary and Maria?" Hazel Dixon asked my mother.

"They're upstairs. We thought it wasn't fair for our kids to come and not others."

"Maybe next year they could come? They're part of the family restaurant. I'd love to see them and I'm sure others would, too." Hazel smiled. Thanks to Hazel, Gary and I attended the annual party in following years. Mother even bought us new party clothes in Great Falls. It was at the 1957 party that my father offered his Cadillac, and my brother as chauffeur, for Hazel and Rolly's fall wedding.

Gene was enjoying a glass of rye and ginger ale in the alcove with the Hansons, Mikkelsons, and McLennans.

"We're going to have some mandolin music and a little skit," Mena Mikkelson informed him. "I asked George Harris to bring his strings and I've written a few lines that Lynne, Ras, and I practised this afternoon. What do you say, Gene? You could be in it if you want. Here's the plot …"

Dean Martin's "Memories Are Made of This" filled the dining room. Then as Dean held the opening notes of "Return to Me," my father put his

Gene and Martha's party for their patrons, April 1954. Caught in the act—Gene is saving Lynne Hanson and Ras Mikkelson from Mena Mikkelson's wrath.

arm around my mother's waist and led her to the dance floor. Although they hadn't danced for a while, they fell naturally into step. Cheek to cheek, Gene sang along softly, "Solo tu, mi amore," only you, my love. The guests clapped and cheered when the song ended. "Kiss her, Gene!" someone shouted and, dipping my mother in his arms, he obliged.

"Ladies and gentlemen," announced Mena. "All the way from England, the world's best mandolin player, George Harris. Okay, George, it's all yours."

Mary's husband, George, didn't come to La Villa very often, but this evening the elfin man took his mandolin from its case, and began plucking a sweet English folk song. George had left England to tour Canada and ended up settling in Calgary in 1920. He had little with him, except for a popular English home remedy that he sold by mail order. Harris Health Wondro Tonic, as he called it, did so well during Prohibition that George produced it locally and invested the profits in the Turner Valley oil fields. The resulting fortune allowed him and Mary to live well, and their daughter, Vera, to pursue flying and trapshooting.

"Now the banjo," friends pleaded. "Play 'Oh Susanna!'" guests shouted and then joined in to sing many choruses.

Swede Hanson stepped forward. "Ladies and gentlemen," he announced. "Mena Mikkelson has written a little play as a present for Martha and Gene. Please welcome Mena and her company."

Mena bounded out of the ladies washroom. "I come to Gene's La Villa all the time with my husband, Ras," she began.

"So do we!" shouted the audience.

"Ya, but I have a problem. I lost him. Where is my handsome man?" Mena put her hand to her brow and scanned the room to see Ras and Lynne Hanson dancing cheek to cheek. As soon as Mena spotted them, she ran for them crying, "Stop canoodling with my husband! I'm going to kill this woman and then you, Ras, my love." Mena wailed and picked up a chair to crush them.

Lynne dropped to her knees to beg that Ras be spared. All of a sudden, my father burst into the scene, cigarette dangling from his mouth, fists up like a boxer. The guests cheered. He told Mena to back off. "No fighting in my restaurant. Get out!" he shouted. Roars of laughter engulfed the dining room.

"Okay, I'll take my husband and leave," Mena sobbed.

"No. He stays," replied Gene. "He's a good customer."

By the time of this party, in spring 1954, Gene had many good customers like Ras. In choosing his villa, he had gambled that his reputation and his business could prosper in the bucolic countryside. His gamble had paid off. The surrounding area was at that very point in time when a nudge of change starts an unalterable process.

La Villa was that nudge.

At the same time that cattle hooves thundered across La Villa grass on the way to different pastures, city council approved the uniquely modern Spruce Cliff Apartments project. Montrealer Stanley Vineberg invested seven million dollars in Hamilton Smith's idea to create a community housed in apartments. Vineberg and Smith believed that some Calgarians would prefer to rent rather than to buy a house.

The Spruce Cliff Apartments were just a half mile north of La Villa. A customer and friend, Bill Bishop, was project manager, and he completed the first apartment building in November 1953. Although there were eighteen more buildings to come, as well as schools, parks, and a shopping area, the opening ceremony for this building was a big political event. Bill ordered his workers to paint the grass emerald green for the occasion when Mayor Don Mackay cut the ribbon. The City was on a spree, selling hundreds of acres around La Villa for housing developments. People living in the Spruce Cliff Apartments and other new communities started coming to La Villa for dinner. It soon became the neighbourhood restaurant, but in this case, the restaurant didn't come to the neighbourhood, the neighbourhood came to the restaurant.

The summer of 1954 was hot and dry. As I looked out the window late one morning, I saw an unusual bright orange sky that confounded me. "Mommy, come and see the beautiful sunset," I called out. To her horror, my mother saw that the barn was on fire and the flames had shot across the dry grass and had started climbing up the restaurant siding. Thick black smoke was already seeping up the stairs. Mother ran to get wet towels to place over our mouths. The window and wall were blistering hot, too dangerous to touch; the smoke now blocked our view. Where was the staircase? Grabbing me, Mother flew to the other end of the hallway. She opened the door to the small second-storey porch. Suddenly we could breathe.

Meanwhile, Father and Gary had stopped for pancakes after their shopping rounds and were speeding home, as usual. As they bombed up the 17th Avenue hill, Gary pointed to black plumes of smoke in the distance. "It's probably the farmers burning off a field," Father replied. As they passed Cuddie's Corner, they heard the screaming sirens, the sky now as black as night. "Son of a bitch!" shouted Father. "La Villa's burning!" He gunned the car. By the time they reached the restaurant parking lot, four fire trucks were sweeping water over one side of the house and the burnt fields where the barn had stood.

"Where are they?" Father shouted. "Where?" Gary pointed to the opposite end of the house. There, climbing down the ladder truck, were a fireman and Mother, carrying me in her arms. Gary took me and my father hugged my mother. "I'm going to build us a house," Gene whispered between sobs.

My father's romantic notion of La Villa as a farm went up in flames with the barn. He realized that owning almost four acres of land in the city's booming southwest was far more lucrative than having a farm. There was now much greater potential to develop plans for the land as well as for La Villa. The city was no longer on our doorstep; the line had moved north with the Spruce Cliff Apartments, the new Spruce Cliff housing subdivision, and the City's annexation of the neighbouring hamlet of Rosscarrock.

My parents were bent on ensuring that La Villa would progress, too.

Family dinner at La Villa to celebrate the visit from Montreal of Frank Santopinto, his wife, Clara, and their children, Rick and Linda, summer 1954.

Bob Templin's plan to build a hotel on the lakefront beside his restaurant in Coeur d'Alene remained fresh in my father's memory. "We have plenty of land, Marta. Let's build a hotel beside the restaurant. When the golf course holds tournaments, players can stay at our hotel. During Stampede the hotel would be full. We'll make a package deal with the oil companies and their visiting executives to stay and eat at La Villa."

"It's a good idea," agreed my mother. "But we need a house first."

"We'll look into both!" my father assured her. "Let's go see some new houses on Sunday, and in the meantime, I'll ask Alderman McIntosh what we have to do to get City permission to build on La Villa property."

Over coffee, Alderman Don McIntosh listened to my father's idea, marvelling at Gene's confidence and tenacity. There was no holding this immigrant back. Don recommended that Gene call the City planning department for advice.

My father paid a visit to the planning department and explained his intention to build a hotel. "There's a problem," the clerk pointed out. "Your land is allocated for agricultural use. You can't build anything commercial." My father noted that his restaurant had already been in operation for two years. The clerk suggested that it might be possible to get a variance, but not now. The planning department was in the process of drawing up the master plan for city development, including the fast-growing southwest area. "Wait until we finish the plan and then come back."

My father was disappointed because once he had an idea, he itched to get started on it immediately. He would have hired Nick to start digging the hotel foundation if he could, and he found it very difficult to wait. "It's okay," my mother said after hearing of the delay. "We'll continue to work on our plans, and when the City's ready, we'll be ready. Let's go see the model homes in Glendale after church on Sunday."

It was only seven blocks from Holy Name Church to Glendale. We looked at some of the Art Sullivan show homes. The new bungalows had oak floors, pastel-coloured bathrooms, lots of kitchen cabinets, and a new kind of aluminum storm window that could be removed with the change of seasons.

"Look." My father pointed to the price on a brochure. It was double what they had paid for La Villa—$1,400 to buy the land and utilities from the City and $14,400 for the custom-built Art Sullivan home, with a $3,000 down payment. My parents looked at each other and then at the steady stream of people interested in the house. Some of the one thousand newcomers to Calgary each month were snapping up these homes.

"Did you like those houses?" Mother asked on the way home.

Teasing her, Father answered, "I liked the chair with the automatic footstool. It's good for watching TV."

Mother's laughter rang through the car.

"Honestly, Marta, I just want one thing—a house that's near La Villa so I can come home and rest and then go back when the restaurant gets busy. You decide what you want inside, that's up to you."

On a snowy November evening in 1954, a couple of months after viewing the show homes, Joe Yurkovich, a builder, came to La Villa for an early dinner. He made straight for the kitchen. "Hi, Gene. I just got a City permit to build a few houses over on 33rd Street and 12th Avenue. I'm taking one for myself. We'll be neighbours."

"Wait a minute! I want Marta to hear."

A moment later he asked the only question that mattered to him: "Could you see La Villa from the corner lot?"

"Sure. It's only a couple of blocks away. It would be the nearest house to the restaurant," said Joe.

"What do you think, Marta?"

"It could work," she said and started asking Joe for details while my father cooked Joe's dinner, on the house.

Meanwhile, at the Spruce Cliff Apartments complex, they had built several more three-storey buildings, and some of the most flamboyant people in Calgary leased them. The renters included oil executives and professionals who had just moved to the city, football and hockey players in town for the season, and young bachelors on the move. Paying ninety-five dollars a month to lease a modern two-bedroom unit with appliances was a good deal for them. In 1955, the new quarterback for the Stampeders, Don Klosterman, arrived in Calgary. First he moved into the Spruce Cliff Apartments, then he dropped in at La Villa for dinner.

The day that Don walked into the restaurant had been a very important day for my father. As a card-carrying Liberal, he had been invited to meet Prime Minister Louis St. Laurent, who was visiting Calgary as part of Alberta's fiftieth anniversary. My father had shaken hands with the prime minister and thanked him for recognizing the commitment, contribution, and patriotism of immigrants such as himself. My father was relating the details of the meeting to Father Tim and Florence Thorpe and didn't notice the new Stampeder quarterback come in. But as soon as my father saw Don sitting alone with his menu, he went over to welcome him and to recommend various items.

"Come, let me introduce you to my friends," Gene offered. Florence was a radio personality, real estate agent, and linchpin of Sacred Heart Parish. The priest invited Don to join their table. Over time, the unlikely combination of the real estate agent, the priest, the quarterback, and the cook became good friends.

Other well-known customers caught my attention. "Do you want me to show you how to twirl your spaghetti on the fork?" I asked tall, blond, handsome Dave Scatcherd, an heir of the Labatt brewery family. Dave later became the host of *Guys and Dolls*, a Saturday afternoon program where teenagers danced to live bands. Now the good-looking fellow was right here in La Villa. Seeing a TV personality in our restaurant was exciting, but I only offered my seven-year-old expertise to those whom I liked. I offered to help handsome Billy Belzberg, too.

"Don't mind my daughter." My mother would smile as she guided me away from my latest student. She knew it was difficult for me to appreciate the line between home and business, living every day in both. Maybe this was another reason why she was looking forward to moving into our new house. It would impose the separation of our family and business life.

In the fall of 1956, we walked down gangplanks scattered across piles of mud and dirt into our finished house. Father ran directly to the large picture window in the front room, while Mother took Gary and me from room to room. She had filled my bedroom with new furniture, and Gary's too, including a large desk where he could do his homework. The bathroom walls were beautiful splattered pink hues, which Mother called Roxitone. Mint green fixtures matched the flecks in the black tile floor. We ended the tour in the living room at the picture window. My father was still looking out. There it was. Gene's La Villa was still standing, without him.

The expanding city limits brought us improved bus service, but I thought that the best development was a new drive-in movie theatre called the 17th Avenue Drive-In. It was only five minutes away. On Sunday, after the restaurant closed, we had just enough time to make it to the drive-in. Gary usually made popcorn and packed bottles of pop, and I put on my pajamas as instructed, grabbing a couple of blankets and a doll. I remember a Sunday evening shortly after my father had bought his new green Packard sedan. The sun was sinking as we roared down the gravel road to get to the drive-in on time. "Do you think we'll make it for the cartoons?" Gary asked.

"What's the movie?" Father shot back. No one knew, but it didn't matter. We were going for the experience of watching a movie outdoors in our new car. We screeched to a halt, joining the lineup to pay. Father drummed his thumb on the steering wheel as we waited, and once inside, he eyed the spot he wanted. Unaccustomed to the larger size of the new car, he rammed the Packard up on the little mound so close to the speaker that he couldn't manoeuvre it off the post, let alone hang it on the window. Struggling mightily in the tight space, he got the large, heavy audio box inside the car and then gingerly put it on the padded leather dashboard. Since the front end of the car sat much higher than the back, I had to climb over the seat and sit between my parents to see.

One block separated business and family life, but it was like living in two different worlds. We had neighbours, so I had kids to play with after school. On Mondays, Mother went shopping. When I came home for lunch, I would often find my father sitting at the kitchen table with a cup of coffee and a cigarette. Rather than making lunch, he would always say, "Let's go out and you can tell me all about school."

There was, however, one occasion, and one occasion only, when my father would cook at home. On Monday afternoons, my father sometimes walked across the street to the Calgary Gun Club to see who was there. At the spur of the moment, he would invite friends home for a buffet, phoning to alert Martha. "Buffet" was my father's term for "cook anything that's in the house and put it on the table." Mother threw the crocheted ecru tablecloth that Aunt Annie had made across the new light oak dining table. On top, she put stacks of Winfield china plates and fanned the stainless silverware in a semicircle, along with thick, white paper napkins.

Rushing home before his friends, Father might beat scrambled eggs and Parmesan cheese into Lipton's chicken noodle soup to make a quick stracciatella. He created bruschetta with chopped tomatoes and garlic on toasted thick-sliced bread. Sometimes he opened cans of chili con carne, maybe adding some ground beef, and served it with garlic toast. Occasionally, some planning went into the "buffet" and then my father might cook French coq au vin or sweet and sour Chinese ribs.

Mother was the one who prepared the family meals at home. Her specialties were the German dishes from her childhood in North Dakota. To Gene's buffet she added browned meat loaf with a little mustard on the side, a cucumber salad dressed in sour cream and dill, and a green salad with the famous La Villa vinaigrette. On Mondays my mother often baked a fruit *kaseküchen*, a German cheesecake made with sweet raised dough. The cottage cheese custard filling, topped with apricots or peaches, was my favourite—it was everyone's favourite! The food served at home was very different from La Villa's menu, but over time the guests got used to seeing Gene and Martha relaxing and entertaining at home.

The buffets were occasions for my parents and their friends to gossip and discuss issues. They talked about Sam Nickle, an oil tycoon, taking his seventeen-member family on a two-month tour of Europe. "They're visiting Rome and Florence," noted my father. "Everyone loves Italy these days." The big discussion, however, centred on the City's plan to buy the Gun Club lands and relocate the club to a property near the airport. My father did not want to lose the business and the camaraderie that had grown between the club members and La Villa, yet he understood that the club occupied thirty acres of increasingly valuable land.

Times were changing, and my father's plans with them. "In addition to a hotel, let's build a new La Villa," he declared. "It'll be modern. I'll bring in good Italian wines. It'll be like a *ristorante* in Italy. A little bit more classy. Once the City approves the rezoning of our property for commercial use, let's build everything new. What could be simpler?"

Hearing that the City's master plan had been completed, my father submitted a proposal to the Technical Planning Board in 1957 for permission to rezone La Villa land to build a hotel and restaurant. Permission was denied on the basis that there was enough commercial development in the area and that the land should be residential.

Gene was perplexed. How could his land be zoned residential when he had a business on the property? My parents discussed the situation. "Go with the simpler plan," advised Mother. "Rebuild La Villa as a modern restaurant and cocktail lounge. We could draw up plans and ask Don McIntosh if he has any helpful information. When we think that the time is right, we'll resubmit the new plan to the City." But my father was very unhappy with the imposed slowdown to his plans. He was used to nudging time, not waiting for it.

La VILLA
THE HOME OF
FINE ITALIAN
DISHES

Thirteen

❧ THE HIGHLIGHT ❧
OF OUR TIME

Gene's La Villa was the
highlight of our time.

—Barbara Bishop

AFTER five years of hard work at La Villa, my parents allowed themselves the luxury of taking more time to enjoy each other and their family. Mother reduced her working hours to just Friday and Saturday nights. On Sundays, when we had family dinner at La Villa, she was a casual hostess, greeting friends and their families.

We still went to La Villa nearly every night. Tuesday to Saturdays, Mother cooked dinner at home and when Gary and I returned from school, we walked with the box of food to the restaurant. Her invention of the "take-in" dinner ensured that we ate together as a family. Afterwards, we went back home to do school work. My father joined us around eight to watch an hour of television together. He kept one eye on La Villa, and if he fell asleep, Mother watched to see if the restaurant got busy. If it did, she woke him; if things were quiet, she let him sleep, but he always kissed me good night, even though it disturbed his nap, because we wouldn't see him until dinner the following night.

Gene was now fifty years old, and Martha often reminded him of the advice he'd given her when they bought their first restaurant: "Who wants to work hard when you're old? Work hard when you're young." It took all her talents to convince him to bring in extra help. He capitulated and hired a sous-chef. After training him for a month, Gene told him, "You can cook the pasta."

My father continued to give time to supporting newcomers from Italy. Shortly after arriving in Riverside, they would learn about

"Mr. Gene" and phone him. "Come to La Villa and have dinner" was always my father's response, and the caller always felt honoured.

Sometimes on a Sunday or right after finishing work during the week, the recently arrived Lino Massolin and my father's friend and *paesano* Lorenzo Ciuffa arrived at La Villa, walking in the back door to greet Gene. My father took out some veal for Milanese, their favourite dish.

Mother, Father, and me surrounded by La Villa staff, 1955.

They sat in the secluded alcove, where speaking Italian wouldn't disturb the customers. My father delivered the veal himself and sat down to visit. "How's it going?" he asked Lino.

"I'm still looking for a full-time job. It's been eight months," replied the handsome young man from Treviso, near Venice. Lino could find only odd jobs—helping at the church or doing cleanup work—which paid sixty-three cents an hour. His share of the monthly rent was ten dollars for the small apartment where he lived with three other bachelors.

Talk turned to their hometowns and to clothes, since both believed in presenting a *bella figura*. Lino had brought fine Italian wool three-piece suits with him, but in Calgary he wore locally bought cheap clothes so that he wouldn't stand out. My father poured some Drambuie into their coffees. "How are things in Riverside?"

"The Hungarian refugees are taking the pressure off us," observed Lino.

"Ya. Marta was reading about different community groups helping them. Calgary is changing. Some people still hate Italians but others love Italy! Have you seen the newspaper ads? 'Come to Italy,' they urge."

"More Italian products, too," laughed Lino. "You can buy a Fiat here. I wonder how many they've sold?"

"Ya, Italy's getting popular," my father agreed. "Safeway has an Italian food section. After seven years, my customers know a lot about Italian food. But Calgarians still have a lot to learn. Some can't think of Italy without thinking about the Mob."

Talk turned to the restaurant business. In response to his questions, Gene told Lino about his passion for cooking and his experiences. "Before I opened an Italian restaurant, I catered Italian food. It's low overhead and good profit. You cook only a few dishes and you know how much to make. It was a good start."

As they were leaving, my father patted Lino's shoulder. "When you find something you like, never give up, but work hard at it, seven days a week."

That Gene had succeeded outside the Italian community impressed Lino, and as a result, the restaurant business now interested him. Lino had wanted to be self-employed and he liked the idea of low costs and high profits from catering. He would get a full-time job, save some money, learn about cooking, and—if Fortuna smiled on him—own a restaurant. Years later, Lino married Norma Ciuffa, and with hard work they eventually owned the successful Romeo and Juliet Restaurant.

Succeeding against the odds was something that my father and Don Klosterman, the Stampeder quarterback, had in common. They appreciated each other's personal stories about struggling to get to the top of their professions. Don had made All-American playing for Loyola in 1951; however, when he entered the professional ranks, Fortuna placed him as the second-string quarterback. Klosterman wasn't one to wait around. He left the champion Los Angeles Rams to get playing time in Calgary. Like my father, Don didn't give up; he was determined to do his best in Calgary and had begun to turn his career around. That's why in 1957 Father Tim's phone call hit hard. "Don Klosterman had a ski accident at Mount Norquay. They don't know if he'll live. He's received last rites."

My father was afraid of sickness and death, having lost both his father and mother at a young age, so he tried not to think about it.

Gary dresses for Stampede, July 1956.

However, he was also concerned about the well-being of his friends, and the grave reports from Father Tim saddened him. A few days later, he got a personal report from Dave Scatcherd, who'd been there on the day of the accident. Dave said that Don was on his last run of the day when suddenly a woman came down the icy slope out of control. To avoid colliding with her, he went over the cliff and smashed into trees. Don had broken nearly every bone in his body. He was paralyzed. My father just shook his head.

One evening, over rigatoni and meatballs, the priest and the cook commiserated on the fate of their friend. "You'd think that in 1957, when rockets are going into space, that the doctors could fix him up but the heat therapy has burned his skin and now he needs skin grafts," said Father Tim, slamming his fork on the table. "Why don't you go visit him, Gene?"

"I can't do that. I hate hospitals. But I can send food. How about you look after his spirit and I'll take care of his body."

"Are you okay, Gene?" the priest asked as he looked into the pale face.

"It's just that talking about this is hard. I'll be thankful when Don comes home."

"Ya. I was thinking how much I have to be thankful for."

My parents were thankful for their good fortune and for the way that Gary was maturing. When Gary turned sixteen and obtained his driver's licence, they bought him a green Morris Minor. The catch was that Gary had to pick up the Unico spaghetti shipments from the train station once a month and look after me on Friday and Saturday nights. Gary's friends were happy to spend those weekend nights at our house. I was usually asleep when they arrived. Around eleven, Mother called from La Villa. "Your snack's ready." My brother picked up Italian rolls stuffed with veal or meatballs, peppers, and mushrooms, a pizza, or spaghetti dinners, and enjoyed a late night TV movie with his friends.

Gary had always done well in school, he even skipped grade two. In grade twelve he was selected as one of four students to represent St. Mary's Boys' High School on the local television program *Reach for the Top*. Leaving the kitchen in staff hands, my parents sat riveted as week after week Gary and his team won, becoming the 1956 champions. The family in Riverside was proud and my parents bragged to customers. Yet soon after the win, Father announced, "Gary should come into the business when he graduates. I'll teach him to cook."

"No! He's not going into the business!" Mother said. "Do you really want our son to work as hard as we have?"

"But he'll just start where we leave off."

"Gary's a good student. He should go to university. It's as simple as that."

Father reluctantly agreed, perhaps with the lingering thought that there was nothing to stop Gary from joining the business after he had his university degree … if he wanted to. In the fall of 1957, Gary entered the first class of the Faculty of Arts and Science at the University of Alberta at Calgary, attending classes in two Quonset huts on the west side of the campus of the Southern Alberta Institute of Technology.

That same fall, my father decided that I had the potential to be an opera singer and enlisted the assistance of his friend Norma Piper Pocaterra, an acclaimed coloratura soprano. He took me to audition for singing lessons and enjoyed a glass of wine with George Pocaterra while I tried my best to impress the kind diva. She agreed to give me lessons, stressing that the voice of a nine-year-old was very young. I'm not sure that my father heard her.

Once a week after school, I walked to the Pocaterra house for my lesson. The diva told me, "If you work hard, your dreams could come

true just as mine did, to study in Milan." It was there that she had met her husband, a rebel from a prominent Italian textile family who had followed his dream to be a cowboy in Alberta. She taught me songs in Italian for the Christmas concert. My beaming father told me, "You sang 'O Solo Mio' better than anyone, *cara*."

"But, Daddy, I was in the chorus."

Also that fall, my father bought a solitaire diamond pinky ring from Bill Belzberg and a two-tone blue 1958 Cadillac with long fins. The immigrant teenager from Antrodoco had arrived, but he wasn't ready to slow down. My father had drawn up plans to build a new La Villa that would be a little more formal, with a list of fine wines, and he also had a budding idea to create and market Gene's frozen spaghetti sauce and meatballs.

He was busy on these new projects in the beginning months of 1958 when he became ill. His stomach pains became frequent and severe enough that he admitted, "Marta, I have to see Doc Gelfand." My mother knew that Gene had a great fear of doctors and hospitals. She said the only words that could ease his fears, "I'll come with you."

"Gallstones," declared Sid Gelfand.

"But, Doc, my mother died of a ruptured gall bladder!"

Seeing the stricken look on his friend's face, Dr. Gelfand added, "Don't worry, Gene. It's a routine operation; you'll be as good as new in a couple weeks."

"Promise that I won't miss more than one Saturday night at La Villa?"

"I'll schedule the surgery to have you back as soon as possible. Oh, I thought that you might like to know that Don Klosterman left the hospital after a year. It's quite amazing. He can walk with just a cane."

My father smiled. Over the months, my father's food had brought strength, and Father Tim's visits, hope. Dr. Gelfand's news made Gene feel that everything would be fine.

The surgery was scheduled for Wednesday, 23 April. Mother invited all our relatives to La Villa for dinner on the Sunday before to celebrate Gene's fifty-first birthday. Gisetta brought his favourite orange chiffon cake. The next day my father decided that the Monday treat would be going out for Chinese food and seeing *The Seven Hills of Rome*, the first wide-screen, CinemaScope movie to be shown in Calgary. When Mario Lanza sang "Arrivederci Roma," my father sobbed.

The next day, Martha washed Gene's back, as she often did, and listened to his instructions. "I'm going to leave my diamond ring here and you can bring it when you pick me up from the hospital. Are you sure that you can handle Saturday night at La Villa by yourself?"

"I'll be fine. Let's just get this over

Gene's photo that was put in La Villa newspaper ads.

with." She packed his suitcase and held him for a long time. She smelled the freshness of his skin and then kissed her partner goodbye.

"One more thing," Father added. "When Maria gets home from school, give her a kiss for me. Tell her I'll see her in a week." Gary backed the Cadillac out of the garage and drove Father to the hospital.

Mother didn't eat that day, or Wednesday either, until Dr. Gelfand phoned to say that the operation was a success. She sang as she made chicken soup to take on her next visit. I was not allowed to go with her and Gary; hospital rules said that as a ten-year-old, I was too young.

On Saturday, Dr. Gelfand phoned early in the morning, "Gene's had a heart attack."

Mother and Gary flew to Father's bedside. "Marta, take me home. I'll die if I stay here."

Mother turned to Dr. Gelfand. "How do we get an ambulance?"

"He's too weak to be moved."

Mother was in a frenzy to find some way to help but on Saturday, 26 April 1958 the happiest period of her life ended.

Aunt Annie and Uncle Manuel were looking after me that day. In the evening they turned on the TV and watched, *Requiem for a Heavyweight*. I found it dark and unsettling and so I was relieved when Gary and my mother returned from the hospital around 9:00 PM. My brother sat me on his knee. Mother whispered, "Your father won't be coming home. He's in heaven with the angels." Saturday night and La Villa was dark.

I took in the words without their meaning. Later, Gary told me, "We have to be brave and help Mother." This I understood. I could try to help my mother and not burden her with my feelings and, of course, not fight with Gary.

The Rowe party sent a spectacular bouquet of fragrant spring flowers. My mother cried, remembering the Cionis' first party at La Villa, and now everything was ending. Uncle Manuel and Aunt Annie moved into our house to try to fill the emptiness, but my father's absence was too large to fill. There were constant visitors, which Gary said "took Mother's mind off of things." I thought it was very strange that people were bringing food to us, but my mother didn't want to cook. She spent much of the time in her bedroom, and when guests dropped by, she spoke with them without smiling. She told me, "There's Mass tomorrow morning. Wear your navy blue clothes. I put them out." I wondered why we would go to Mass in the middle of the week, but I wasn't going to burden anyone with questions.

A large black Cadillac that my father would have liked picked us up at the house and took us to Holy Name Church. When we arrived, the crowd parted to let the car park in front of the church, then closed around my mother. Mother held our hands, keeping us close. Father Tim was the first to hug each of us, and he stayed with us throughout the morning, often holding Mother's arm. I saw Dr. Gelfand, a man who had bandaged and nursed me, a man who always comforted our family. Today, he was crying. I watched him pat his eyes with his handkerchief and heard him whisper to my mother, I lost a dear friend.

Inside, the church was packed, but seats had been saved at the front for us, with Auntie Gisetta and my cousins, Jean, Jack, Connie, and Nino, and my mother's family. I sat between Mother and Gary and watched the priest circle the coffin, but my mind refused to think what was inside. The friends and patrons from Saturday night at La Villa were there to be with Gene for one last time.

The police who directed the funeral traffic were my father's friends. They looked sad to see that Gene had stopped, not just slowed down. I noticed that the grass at the cemetery was green and the birds were singing—my father loved spring, when life began again. Afterwards, we joined relatives and friends at home and had a very simple buffet of cold cuts and buns.

My father had no will. He either thought that it was too soon to consider his death or else he felt that making a will was asking for bad luck. My mother was left with a few thousand dollars in the bank, his diamond ring, and the 1958 Cadillac. She put the ring away in the safety deposit box at the bank and sold the car immediately. She told herself that she didn't have the luxury of time to grieve, she needed to make money to support her family. She opened La Villa three weeks later. Through the spring and summer, my mother made the spaghetti sauce. "Thank God I know the recipe," she muttered each day. Gary did the shopping. The sous-chef did much of the cooking under my mother's eagle eye.

In August, Gary asked, "Shall I quit university to help you?"

"No. We want you to go back."

That fall, when Gary went to Edmonton for his second year of university, Uncle Manuel and Aunt Annie moved in with us and we established a home routine that simultaneously comforted and numbed. In December, I sang along with the Christmas carols, not knowing that it made my mother want to smash the radio. During the Christmas holidays, she asked Gary to transfer for his third year back to Calgary. She needed to have her children near.

My mother knew that Gene was to La Villa as tomatoes are to spaghetti sauce, but she needed the restaurant income. A cook named Joe Di Palma approached her to run the restaurant. He was an experienced cook, but I think it was his wife, Rita, and two little boys who clinched her decision. They were a young family, just as we had been, and like us they would live above the restaurant.

Joe soon realized that he was in my father's shadow, but he held on for nearly two years, doing his best to compete with new restaurants that had liquor licences. Finally, Mother decided to close the restaurant before things got worse. She wanted their customers to remember Gene's La Villa as the highlight of their times.

"How can we help you?" friends and patrons asked Mother.

"Buy La Villa," she replied wryly.

Months later, in the fall of 1959, Ab McDonald, a friend of Sam Ross, and John Zaozirny, a businessman with interests in the Imperial Hotel, made her an offer on behalf of their group to buy La Villa land in order to build a hotel. The Dinosaur Hotel, as they thought to call it, would be the first hotel beer parlour and lounge in southwest Calgary. Mother smiled at the thought that Gene's vision of a restaurant and hotel complex had been right on target.

There was a small catch: the deal was contingent on rezoning the property for commercial use. My mother would have to succeed with rezoning permission where my father had failed.

The proposal to rezone La Villa land passed first reading on 15 February 1960. It was Gary who stood by Mother, as his father had before him, and helped her to prepare a statement for second reading, held three weeks later in public. Although Mother and Gary arrived early at city council chambers, it took awhile to find seats together. Gary was reading aloud the names of the twelve opposing petitions on the agenda when suddenly Mother clasped his arm. "Oh my God, our next door neighbours! They're against us, too."

Mother twisted her hanky around her finger to control her emotions and concentrate on the facts. There were three main reasons why various groups opposed the rezoning: the presence of a beer parlour within a mile of a few schools, a preference for an athletic centre rather than a hotel, and the concern of local merchants that they would have to compete with more businesses attracted to the area. The merchants had become nervous when in mid-November 1959, Jack Barron, owner of the 17th Avenue Drive-In, announced a potential multi-million dollar mall development to counter the proposed Dinosaur Hotel.

"Mrs. Cioni, it's your turn," directed Mayor Hays.

In a trembling voice she began to read from the podium. "In 1951, Gene and I, with our family, moved into what is known as Gene's La Villa. We lived there so we could devote all our time to our business. It was tough and hard going. We worked eighteen hours a day. We had a coal furnace, propane gas, a well, and no transportation as late as 1953 … Now, after running a very successful business for nine and a half years, others who came so much later than we are trying to force us out. This land … lying at least two blocks from the closest inhabitants, has been commercial for the last nine and a half years."

The chamber was silent as Mother sat down. City council voted 6 to 3 to pass second reading. That should have been the end of the debate, but the press, civic reformers, community and school associations, churches, and residents in southwest Calgary were up in arms, contending that city council had set aside the master plan in order to rezone Gene's La Villa. For three months, the city's action became THE public issue, and the derogatory term "spot" rezoning was coined to ignite and coalesce opposition.

In an unprecedented response, city council permitted a second public hearing. Mother's initial optimism plummeted when she received the notice, and she glanced at the little bluebird of happiness above the kitchen door frame. "Gene, please help me. I need strength."

Opponents rallied to produce one large petition. As my mother went about her daily routine, getting me off to school, shopping, visiting Joe at La Villa, she would pass volunteers going from house to house to collect signatures against her rezoning application. Five days before the second public hearing, four hundred protesters assembled at Melville Scott School, near our house. "Let's go see what they're up to," Mother urged Gary. They huddled near the back and were shocked when the four city councillors were booed each time they tried to speak.

On 21 March, hundreds came to fight city hall, presenting the largest petition ever—2,447 signatures. Mayor Hays directed that four could speak against and two for the rezoning. First, however, the city planner presented the facts, pointing out that a new four-lane highway, the Banff Coach Road, would circle La Villa land, making it unsuitable for residential use, as had been envisaged in 1957.

Gary and Mother listened as Alderman McIntosh forced the Calgary School Board to acknowledge that schoolchildren had been given rezoning protest petitions to take home for their parents' signatures. Alderman Mary Dover offered that she knew a person who had been asked to sign the petition seven times. Alderman Mack, still seething from the hecklers' abuse at the school meeting, told residents that their arguments "didn't hold too much water," adding that they were "emotionally disturbed."

Stella Volk, the former La Villa head waitress, rose to speak in favour of the rezoning, and then Mother spoke last.

"I had no idea of coming back, but I think it only fair that you be presented with my side of the argument. It was stated that the area in question be used for a hospital, recreation centre, park, or similar endeavour [but] how can my land be included in any of these plans [with] a four-lane highway [nearby]? ... I see where the opposition has brought in communities as far away as Briar Hill. If Briar Hill can exert influence to stifle commercial development throughout the city, then it will be a sad outlook for businesses, both big and small, of this city.

"I cannot afford to keep this land idle and pay taxes on it as it is the only livelihood for myself and my children. If Gene were here he would likely have his own new dining room and cocktail lounge on this site and continue to serve the public with the same high standards as he had done for the past twenty-five years."

The mayor called for a vote. Council approved the rezoning of La Villa by a 6 to 4 decision.

Within three months, La Villa was boarded up, awaiting demolition. Looking out the picture window in our front room, Mother said to Gary and me, "What a dilapidated eyesore! It looks just like we found it ten years ago." Even so, Mother took comfort that it wasn't the building that patrons and friends remembered; it was being with Gene, which was a highlight of the Fabulous Fifties.

FORTUNA forced Gary to grow up quickly. He chose a legal career, influenced as a teenager by prominent lawyers such as D. Austin Lane, a well-dressed, erudite gentleman who thoughtfully set aside his reading to talk to Gary as they waited for the bus, and La Villa patrons Harold Riley, who had helped secure Gene's name, and W. Ken Moore, former Stampeder football player and legal star. Gary's talent and Fortuna's timing led to his appointment as sheriff of Edmonton at age twenty-six. At thirty-one, he became the youngest Alberta provincial court judge. Father would have chuckled proudly at the irony. "And to think that I wanted my son in the restaurant business!"

It was Gary's suggestion to make the trip to Antrodoco that our father would have taken had he lived long enough. Eight years after his death, in May 1966, the Cioni family arrived in Rome. Gene's brother Sabatino had made a life here with his wife, Ida, and their two children, and now their children's families. I'd never seen a photo of Uncle Sabatino, or Zio, as we called him, so when he opened the door, my heart stopped. I looked into my father's large, milky-brown eyes and grinned to see that familiar face again. He kissed my cheeks and I hugged him. Zio was slimmer than my father and had more hair. Zio was quieter—he smiled when my father would have laughed, he stood back rather than led, and his pace was slower. My father sped through his days like a Ferrari race car; Sabatino took his life in stride like a distance marathoner.

Four days later, we journeyed to Antrodoco in time to join hundreds of people lining the streets to pay homage as the villagers carried

A postcard thanking Genesio for his contribution to the
Feast of the Madonna del Grotto, 1930.

The Feast of the Madonna del Grotto, Antrodoco, 1929.

the Madonna from the mountain for her annual visit. My father had told me so many stories about Maria, the Madonna of the Grotto, that for a while she replaced Little Red Riding Hood as my favourite heroine. Children, dressed in First Communion whites, were the same age as I had been when my father died. Solemn-suited men, many the size and shape of my father, carried a large wooden platform on their shoulders. On top, the Virgin Mary floated toward the church, smiling benignly as though she was as pleased to be in Antrodoco as we were.

Zio Sabatino took us on a tour of the town. We started on Via Cutilia, one of the original cobblestone streets that wound between rows of three-storey stone houses. We stopped at number 32, the house where he and my father were born. The tall windows on the second and third floors were similar to the bedroom windows at La Villa. Here, the creamy lace curtains waved out the windows to greet us. Pots overflowed with red geraniums trailing from the balcony and down the front of the house, celebrating the day.

Zio led the way to the railway station. Corso Roma was as old as Via Cutilia, but wider. As we walked downhill, we caught a glimpse of the Velino River and the bridge to L'Aquila. Then Sabatino stopped and pointed. "There's the station where Genesio left."

That's when we noticed the frail old man, dressed in a brown suit and hunched over a cane, standing at the edge of our group. Gary had seen the old man trailing us through town like a shadow; Zio told us who he was. "That's the uncle who took your father to the boat in Naples." The shadow tipped his fedora and smiled. We waved. He was silent, too shy to speak, like a ghost of the family past watching a family future. The uncle could never have known when he nudged the scared teenager into the passenger line in Naples that my father would turn from immigrant to entrepreneur to celebrity chef, all in thirty-five short years, and that my father would introduce a Canadian city to the tastes and culture of this town. He had launched Genesio on a life lived at top speed to an early death, and yet he had remained in the same place, a marker of time.

Zio Sabatino (right) tells the occupant that this house was the Cioni family home.

THOUGHTS AND THANK YOUS

I LEFT Calgary in 1970 to earn my doctorate in history at Cambridge University and afterwards settled in Ontario. I returned annually to Calgary to visit my family, otherwise luring my mother on holidays with me. In 1979, I married Mark Lewis, a communications lawyer, at Gary's house, with my brother officiating. When our daughter, Rafaela, was born in 1988, it became important that she know her Calgary family, so we visited more regularly. It was good planning, for Rafi came to know her Grandma Martha in the five years before my mother died at the age of eighty-three. She was vibrant nearly to the end. "I could go shopping or I could pay for a psychiatrist," Mother told us. "I'd prefer to go shopping."

The year 2002 was my Italian year. I was at the University of Bologna, invited by Professor Vita Fortunati for a week's celebration of the fruitful academic partnership between her famed institution and York University, where I was head of the international office. In a month, I would be leaving York, and I had been contemplating writing my father's story. Each day in Bologna made my decision clearer. Bologna, the gastronomic capital of Emilia Romagna, recalled the importance of food in Italian culture and helped me appreciate the missionary zeal of my father to win the palates of Calgarians.

One day, I went to Venice with Professor Ron Pearlman, another member of the York delegation. "I hear you're from Calgary," he said as the train pulled out of the station. "So am I." Ron's father had owned the company that supplied 7-Up to my father's restaurants, and his parents had spent many Saturday nights at La Villa.

"I've decided to write the story and take Italian lessons," I confided to my friend Elena Lamberti, who taught North American literature at the University of Bologna. She hugged me goodbye at the airport. "*Buona Fortuna!*" she said, slipping the libretto of *The Girl from the Golden West* under my arm.

Fortuna indeed. A week after leaving York, I was in Calgary for the celebration of the fiftieth anniversary in the priesthood of my cousin Magi Santopinto. Family gathered for the occasion, as well as members of the Italian community; it was the ideal time to begin. Gary was excited about and supportive of this project from the start and wrote a time frame of the main events in our parents' lives. In addition to his birth, he listed father's various jobs, illnesses, and restaurants. He contacted friends to pick up our father's trail and endured my endless questions. This is as much his book as mine.

With Gary's recall and perception and my own memories, I thought that I knew my father well, but I would be astounded to find out how much I didn't know. I have been uncovering the facts and details of this story for three years. I am truly grateful to the Mariano A. Elia Chair and Research Fund in Italian-Canadian Studies at York University, Toronto, for research grants and confirming the value of this project.

I made many visits to Calgary to cull the newspaper collection at the University of Calgary Library, find documents in the City of Calgary, the Glenbow Museum, and the Calgary Library Main Branch, seek out

and interview my father's customers and their children, reconnect with the Italian community of my childhood, and find experts such as Stephanie White, who wrote her master's thesis in urban planning on the
Spruce Cliff Apartments.

I had the luxury of interviewing Gisetta's children, my eldest cousins—Connie, Father Magi, and
Nino—on several occasions. They peeled the layers of their memories. Nino, the veteran war photographer,
gave me photos. I had scheduled a second visit with him, but he died the day before. His daughters, Marianne
and Joan, insisted that we finish sorting through his photos, and so Gary and I, with our cousins Jackie and
Gabrielle, brought a few bottles of wine to toast the life of their talented father as we delved into his work.
Cousins on my mother's side, Marsha Massie, Sam and Goldie's daughter, and Martha Brooks, Marion and
Annie's child, spent many hours recalling early family history.

I have lost family during this project, but I have also found some. After thirty years I located my cousin
Susie, Nick Corradetti's daughter, as well as the Poscente family, formerly of Antrodoco and Trail, British
Columbia, now scattered in Toronto, Calgary, and Victoria. Dante Poscente's memories of my father staying
with his family in Trail in the mid-1930s were news to me, and the photo that Dante provided of his brother
Tony with my father is one of my pictorial treasures. Dante introduced me to his niece, Valerie Sovran
Mitchell, a food writer, and I have since found out that the Poscentes are cousins.

Most surprising though was discovering my grandmother, Flavia Cardellini Cioni Corradetti. Until
recently I didn't even know her name, but Fortuna brought me into contact with the relatives of Annibale
Corradetti's third wife, and they provided the timeline for his marriage to my grandmother, as a start.

There are still Antrodocani living in Calgary. I was honoured to sit at the Brandelli family table, learning
from Adelmo the layout of my father's first restaurant and from Gabriele, Adelmo's brother, many details
of post-war Antrodoco. Gabriele's wife, Rita, remembered the opening of Father's second restaurant and
organized an afternoon with many Manzara family members. Lina Cioni Fuxa recalled the close friendship
between our fathers. I had the good fortune to interview others from the older Italian community, such as
Audrey Forzani, Mary Cioni, and Bill Galiardi, who recounted stories for both Gary and me. Mary Comella
told about coming to Calgary from Toronto in the late 1940s and the Sacred Heart Church gang who frequented her grocery store and La Villa.

I found restaurant patrons and their families—Rolly Bradley, Barbara Bishop, Hy and Jenny Belzberg,
Ron Holdsworth and his Aunt Helen, Bob Rowe, John Hanson, Phyllis Gelfand, and Sugarfoot Anderson
(to name a few), who in turn led me to many others. I phoned La Villa devotees scattered throughout Canada
and the United States and listened to their stories.

As a trained historian, I rejoiced to find key photos in the collections of Tony and Nina Valerio, Barbara
Bishop, my cousin Gisele Amantea, and Ezio Carloni in Antrodocco. With the aid of Rocco Maragna, I made
contact with Mayor Dott. Paolo Mannetti and Police Captain Mario Pascasi of Antrodoco to obtain birth,
death, and marriage certificates. Fortuna intervened when I met Maria Coletta McLean, author of *My Father
Came from Italy*. She took me under her wing and into her writers' group with Ann Shortell, Janet Looker,
Netta Rondinelli, and Bryna Wasserman. Their insight and suggestions underpin this book.

I wish to thank Charlene Dobmeier, publisher of Fifth House, for her interest and openness;

Lesley Reynolds, my editor, for her incisive and respectful suggestions; and Meaghan Craven, managing editor and a gentle shepherd.

I realize now that it has been bewildering and even unsettling for my husband, Mark, and daughter, Rafaela, to witness my transformation from a bustling senior manager into a writer fixated with this project, but they gave their love, and I thank them for enduring the journey with me.

Even though I have bookshelves and file drawers of documents, I know that there is information that I did not find. I welcome anyone with recollections of my parents and stories about La Villa to contact me through Fifth House Publishers.

SOURCES

Primary

Alberta Government Services Registries

Antrodoco church archives

L'Aquila Provincial Archives

The City of Calgary Archives

The Calgary Public Library Local History Collection

The Glenbow Museum Archives

Ellis Island Records

Gastronomica: The Journal of Food and Culture. University of California Press: Berkley.

Henderson's Directory Calgary

National Archives of Canada

St. Mary's Cemetery Archives

Statistics Canada

University of Calgary Library, newspaper collection: *The Calgary Herald* and *The Albertan* (1947–1960)

Printed

Batterberry, Michael and Ariane. *On the Town in New York.* New York: Routledge, 1999.

Callen, Anna Teresa. *Food and Memories of Abruzzo Italy's Pastoral Land.* New York: Hungry Minds, 1998.

Capatti, Alberto, and Massimo Montanari. *Italian Cuisine: A Cultural History.* New York: Columbia University Press, Translation 2003.

Chatto, James. *The Man Who Ate Toronto.* Toronto: Macfarlane Walter & Ross, 1998.

Culos, Ray. *Vancouver's Society of Italians.* Madeira Park, B.C.: Harbour Publishing, 2 vols., 1998.

Erb, Marsha. *Stu Hart: Lord of the Ring.* Toronto: ECW Press, 2002.

Fanella, Antonella. *With Heart and Soul: Calgary's Italian Community.* Calgary: University of Calgary Press, 1999.

Flandrin, Jean-Louis, and Massimo Montanari. *A Culinary History of Food.* New York: Columbia University Press, 1999.

Klassen, Henry C. *A Business History of Alberta.* Calgary: University of Calgary Press, 1999.

Lawrence, D. H. *Studies in Classic American Literature.* Cambridge: Cambridge University Press, 2003.

McFadden, Cyra. *Rain or Shine.* New York: Alfred A. Knopf, 1986.

McLean, Maria Coletta. *My Father Came from Italy.* Vancouver: Raincoast Books, 2000.

Milton, John. *Paradise Lost.* http://www.online-literature.com/milton/paradiselost/8/

Mitchell, Valerie. *Polenta On the Board.* Victoria: www.polenta.ca, 2003.

Norberg-Schulz, Christian. *Genius Loci: Towards a Phenomenology of Architecture.* New York: Rizzoli International Publications, Inc., 1980.

Palmer, Howard. *Alberta: A New History.* Edmonton: Hurtig Publishers: 1990.

Palmer, H., and T., eds. *Peoples of Alberta: Portraits of Cultural Diversity.* Saskatoon: Western Producer, 1985.

Prezzolini, Giuseppe. *Maccheroni & C.* Milan: Rusconi, 1998.

Serventi, Silvano, and Françoise Sabban. *Pasta: The Story of a Universal Food.* New York: Columbia University Press, 2000.

Silone, Ignazio. *The Abruzzo Trilogy.* Vermont: Steerforth Press, Translation 2000.

Strode, Woody. *Gold Dust.* Lanham, Maryland: Madison Books, 1990.

Tollis, Camillo. *Profilo Storico di Antrodoco.* Pescara: La Regione, 1980.

Trail of Memories: Trail, B.C. 1895–1945. Altona, Manitoba: Friesens Corporation History Book Division, 1997.

Visser, Margaret. *Much Depends on Dinner.* Toronto: HarperPerennial Canada, 2000.

Visser, Margaret. *The Rituals of Dinner.* Toronto: HarperPerennial Canada, 2000.

White, Stephanie. *The Colonial, the Modern and the National Project, Chapter 2, Spruce Cliff Apartments.* University of British Columbia Dissertation, unpublished.

Wood, Patricia. *Nationalism from the Margins: Italians in Alberta and British Columbia.* Montreal: McGill-Queen's Press, 2002.

Interviews

Amantea, Connie
Amantea, Mike
Anderson, Ezzret (Sugarfoot)
Belzberg, Hy
Belzberg, Jenny
Bishop, Barbara
Bradley, Rolly
Brandelli, Adelmo
Brandelli, Aurora
Brandelli, Gabriele
Brandelli, Jean
Brandelli, Rita
Brooks, Marina (Arndt)
Caracciolo, Nick
Cardellini, Quinto
Cioni, Gary
Cioni, Mary
Ciuffa, Lorenzo
Cohen, Geneva (Grassi)
Comella, Mary
Culos, Ray
Enns, Gabrielle (Amantea)

Finch, Tony
Forzani, Audrey
Fuxa, Lina (Cioni)
Gelfand, Phyllis
Gilliardi, Bill
Hanson, John
Holdsworth, Helen
Holdsworth, Ron
Hryhor, Theresa
Jenkins, Bob
Kalef, Sandy
Keller, Norma Gouldie
Kleiner, Jackie (Amantea)
Koloff, Millie
Kuri, Connie (Santopinto)
Kuri, Frank
Lear, Betty
Manzara, Angela
Manzara, Arnold
Manzara, Carlo
Manzara, Gerry
Manzara, Joe

Massie, Marsha (Ross)
Massolin, Lino
Miotti, Louie
Miotti, Sylvia
Monroe, Effie
Montgomery, Susan (Corradetti)
Pearlman, Ron
Perovich, Dolores (Pini)
Poscente, Dante
Poscente, Gino
Poscente, Julio
Rowe, Bob
Santopinto, Father Magi
Santopinto, Nino
Scatcherd, David
Serani, Peter
Sovran, Eleanor (Poscente)
Talbot, Barbara
Valerio, Nina Carloni
Valerio, Tony
Van Ostrand, Lola
White, Stephanie